Al-Munabbihat
The Counsel

OTHER TITLES IN THIS SERIES

Deliverance from Error and
The Beginning of Guidance
IMAM AL-GHAZALI
Translated by W. Montgomery Watt

|

The Alchemy of Happiness
IMAM AL-GHAZALI
Based on translation by Claude Field

|

Faith Versus Materialism:
The Message of Surat al-Kahf
SAYED ABUL HASAN ALI NADWI
Translated by Mohiuddin Ahmad

|

Surah Ya Sin:
Text, Translation and Commentary
COMPILED FROM VARIOUS SOURCES

|

For details, please visit www.ibtbooks.com

AL-MUNABBIHAT

The Counsel

Ibn Hajar al-Asqalani

Translated and edited by Habib Siddiqui

© Dr Habib Siddiqui 2007

ISBN 978 967 5062 01 8

Published 2007
Islamic Book Trust
607 Mutiara Majestic
Jalan Othman
46000 Petaling Jaya
Selangor, Malaysia

Website: www.ibtbooks.com
Email: ibtkl@streamyx.com

Printed by
Academe Art and Printing Services
Kuala Lumpur

*To my parents
Nazrul Islam and Khadija Siddiqui,
without whose encouragement
I would never have accomplished much,
including writing this book.*

CONTENTS

Translator's Introduction	ix
Glossary of Arabic Terms	xvii
Chapter 1	1
Chapter 2	2
Chapter 3	10
Chapter 4	35
Chapter 5	55
Chapter 6	69
Chapter 7	80
Chapter 8	87
Chapter 9	90
Chapter 10	94

TRANSLATOR'S INTRODUCTION

Praise be to Allah, the Lord of the universe. Peace and blessings be upon His Messenger, Muhammad Ahmad al-Mustafa, who was sent for guidance of humanity, and his family and companions.

It is a great blessing of Allah to be able to present an English translation of the book, *al-Munabbihat*, or the Counsel, to our English readers. I first came across this book while visiting Bangladesh in 1991. The book was published in 1977 by Baitus Sharaf, Chittagong, and contained the original Arabic side by side its Bengali translation by (late) Mawlana Muhammad Abdul Jabbar, a well-known man of *tasawwuf*. In his preface, the translator wrote, "Ten years ago, while I was employed as an instructor at the reputed Wazedia Aliyah Madrasa, Panchlaish, Chittagong,

I was also the Imam for regular prayers at Asghar Ali Sowdagar mosque in Khandaquia village of Hathazari thana. In that mosque after reading the book, I felt the urge to translate the book into Bengali so that it could benefit pious Muslim brothers and sisters. The book is full of many virtuous sayings and words of advice from our Prophet (s), the righteous caliphs, scholars and spiritual guides." After reading the book, like its Bengali translator, I, too, became convinced that *al-Munabbihat* needed to be translated for wider audience. I quickly did a computer search to check if it had been translated into English, and when the result of the search came out negative, I embarked on the task of translating this masterpiece into English.

There seems to be some controversy surrounding the authorship of the book. Most of the extant manuscripts give the impression that the author was Imam al-Hafiz al-Muhaddith Ibn Hajr al-Asqalani (773-852 AH), the great scholar of Islam who lived in Egypt. Shaykh Muhammad Nawawi ibn 'Umar al-Jawi wrote a commentary on the book titled *Nasa'ih al 'Ibad* in 1311 AH, in which he, too, mentioned Ibn Hajr al-Asqalani (may Allah have mercy on him) as the author of this work. The Bengali translated version of Mawlana Abdul Jabbar also attributed its authorship to the famous scholar Ibn Hajr.

Hajji Khalifa (1017/1608 - 1067/1656 AH/AD) in his Arabic bibliographical work on Arabic, Turkish and Persian works and authors, *Kashf al-Zunun* (2:1848) mentions the author of the original work *Munabbihat 'ala al-Isti'dad li-Yawm al-Ma'ad lil-Nus-hi wal-Widad* ("Admonitions for Preparation for the Day of the Return for Advice and Love") as Zayn al-Qudat Ahmad bin Muhammad al-Hijji (or al-Hajri or Hujuri). The catalogue of Arabic manuscripts of the library of Sarajevo (Number 334) also records it as such. It is possible that other manuscripts misattributed the authorship by mixing up the surname with the more famous Imam Ibn Hajr after Hajji Khalifa's death. This conclusion is further evidenced by the fact that Imam Shams al-Din Muhammad bin 'Abd al-Rahman al-Sakhawi (831/1428–902/1497 AH/AD), the foremost student of the Imam, did not include *Munabbihat* in his catalogue of Ibn Hajr's works in *al-Jawahir wa al-Durar fi Tarjamat Shaykh al-Islam Ibn Hajr* (al-Asqalani)

The Counsel

(Pearls and Diamonds: The Biography of Shaykh al-Islam Ibn Hajr of 'Asqalan).

Little else is known about Zayn al-Qudat Ahmad bin Muhammad al-Hijji (or al-Hajri or Hujuri). However, from the internal evidences within the book, it seems that he must have lived after the middle of the 3rd century AH and surely before Hajji Khalifa's death in the 11th century AH. Following the narrative tradition of many Sufi composers, including Imam al-Ghazali (may Allah have mercy on him), the author does not provide the entire chain of narrators but merely mentions the source of his quoted sayings. He might as well have been a Sufi and must have composed the work for wider use among the adepts of the esoteric, kernel, Sufi ways of Islam.

Standing over the carcass of western humanism, with its deadly attachment and preference for the lowly materialism, modern man is gradually stripping himself of spirituality. He has forgotten that he is not just composed of flesh and blood, but also of *nafs* (soul, carnal self) and *ruh* (spirit). Man's genuine humanity lies in subduing the carnal self, in order to uplift the spirit, and not in being enslaved by the former.

Just as a plant needs both water and air for its mere survival, modern man has failed to realize that he needs spiritual nourishment alongside materialism. Who can also deny the fact that while most religions are waging a losing battle today against the influence of materialism many western religions are failing terribly in saving their people from its deadly embrace? That is why, in recent years, many westerners have turned to the Eastern traditions in the hope of reviving their spirits, which they have lost, and correct the deep spiritual and psychic vacuum. It is there that this book is highly recommended for anyone seeking to find that missing equilibrium in his/her life.

True to its name, the book is a collection of wise sayings and words of advice and warnings to prepare the believer for meeting the Lord (*Rabb*) on the Day of Resurrection. As such, it is notable for its reliance on explicitly Islamic materials, and its admonishing and inspirational tone for spiritual elevation. What sets it apart from many other Islamic books is that it is full of wisdom, comprising sayings of the fountainhead of knowledge, Muhammad (*s*), the first four caliphs Abu Bakr, 'Umar, 'Uthman and 'Ali (*r.a.*) and many of the ascetics, Sufis and wise men of the first three centuries of Islam, all put together in two to ten sentences in a small book of this size, and yet so rich with its spiritual nourishment to help anyone to complete the spiritual journey.

It is this fact, in spite of the book's controversial authorship, which testifies to its wide popularity among Muslims for the last several centuries, with translated copies available in most languages of the Muslim people. Truly, anyone who opens any page of this book and reads any sentence is sure to benefit from its teachings. In this age of self-help books, the publication of this book is timely and helpful to develop and strengthen one's faith in God.

I wish to acknowledge the assistance I have received from Dr Shayela Mian Ahmed (previously with the Purdue University) who kindly reviewed my translated work and made valuable suggestions.

I am also grateful to Eva, Hassan and Husayn, who have patiently endured my lengthy involvement in this project. Finally, special thanks to Islamic Book Trust, Kuala Lumpur, for publishing this book, without which many English readers would have been deprived of the opportunity to read this valuable, classical work of Arabic and get a taste of the rich spiritual world of Islam.

I pray and hope that this book serves to fulfill the goal for which it was intended. *Amin.*

Habib Siddiqui
September 2007

GLOSSARY OF TERMS

'abdal	devotee
'abid	worshipper
adab	manners
'adl	justice
akhawah	alms-giving
akhirah	Hereafter or Next world
'alim	religious scholar
'amal	deeds
'arif	gnostic
'aql	intelligence, wisdom
'arsh	Throne
awliya'	friends or patrons
din	religion
dirham	silver coin used as currency
du'a	supplication
dunya	this world
fakhr	pride
faqih	jurist (pl. *fuqaha*)
faqr	poverty
fard	compulsory
fasad	corruption

The Counsel

fasiq	transgressor, froward folk
faqah	starvation, hardship
fawahishah	lewdness
fikr	inner contemplation
fiqh	jurisprudence
fitnah	troubles, disturbance, mischief, persecution, sedition
fitrah	a fixed charity given before Eid-ul-Fitr
fuqara'	dervishes, the poor
ghadab	anger, wrath
gharib	rare, helpless, stranger
ghina	richness
hadith	saying or deed of Prophet Muhammad (pl. *ahadith*)
hafiz	one who memorizes the Qur'an
hajj	pilgrimage
hakim	judge
halal	lawful or permissible
hamd	praise
haram	unlawful or forbidden
hasad	envy
hawa'	passion
haya'	shyness, modesty
Hijri/Hijrah	Islamic calendar, begins with the migration of Prophet Muhammad from Makkah to Madinah
hikmah	genuine wisdom

AL-MUNABBIHAT

hur	companions in Paradise
Iblis	Satan
'ibadah	worship
iffah	chastity
ihsan	generosity
Injil	Scripture revealed to Prophet 'Isa (Jesus) *'alayhissalam*
'ilm	knowledge
imam	leader
'iman	faith or belief
istita'ah	vigor
jama'ah	gathering
Jibril	Angel Gabriel
jihad	striving, holy war
jumu'ah	day of gathering, Friday
jud	liberality
kafn	burial shroud
kalam	theology
khalwah	seclusion
khiyanah	betrayal, treachery
khushu'	humility or humbleness
makhluq	creation
mal	wealth
ma'rifah	gnosis
miskin	needy
Misr	Egypt
miswak	brushing the teeth with a tooth stick

The Counsel

Mizan	Balance
mubah	permissible
muhaddith	scholar of Hadith
Muharram	the first month in the Arabic calendar
mu'min	faithful believer (pl. *mu'minin*)
munafiq	hypocrite
munajah	supplication
mutaqqi	God-fearing (pl. *mutaqqin*)
nar	Fire
nadamah	distress or contrition
nafs	soul, carnal self
qadi	judge
qadr	decree of Allah
qalb	heart
qana'ah	contentment in little
Qiyamah	Day of Judgment
rahah	comfort
rak'ah	units of prayer
Ramadan	month of fasting in the Arabic calendar
rida	pleasure
riya	pride or arrogance
ruh	spirit
sabr	patience
sadaqah	charity or alms-givings
salam	peace
salah	prayer
salih	righteous (pl. *salihun*)

AL-MUNABBIHAT

shahwah	lust
Sha'ban	a month in the Arabic calendar
Shafi'i	one of the four Sunni schools of thought in Islam
al-Sham	Syria
Shari'ah	Islamic Law
sharif	respectable person
shafa'ah	intercession
shukr	gratitude
sirat	bridge over the Hell to Paradise in the Hereafter
sultanah	authority
sunnah	custom, mode operandi, practice (usually referring to those of Muhammad *salla Allahu 'alayh wasallam*)
ta'ah	obedience
taqdir	decree of Allah
tama'	greed
taqwa	fear of Allah
Tawrah	Torah revealed to Prophet Musa, *'alayhissalam*
tawbah	repentance
tawfiq	success
'ulama'	scholars of religion (pl. *'alim*)
ummah	community
uns	fellowship

The Counsel

ushr	a tax of one-tenth fraction on agricultural produce
wudu'	ablution
wali	friend or patron (pl. *awliya'*)
wara'	piety
yaqin	certitude of faith
yatim	orphan
Zabur	Psalms as revealed by Allah to Prophet Dawud, *'alayhissalam*
zahid	ascetic
zakat/zakah	poor-due
zalim	evil-doer (pl. *zalimin*)
zikr	remembrance
zuhud	ascetic detachment

1

All praise is due to Allah, the Beneficent, the Merciful. May the peace and blessings of Allah be upon our leader Muhammad (*salla Allahu 'alayhi wasallam*), his descendants and his Companions!

2

Two good qualities are most virtuous for men: one of these is to have *iman* (faith) in Allah, and the other is to be of service or help to Muslims. And there are two bad qualities that are most harmful to human beings: one of these is to associate anything as a partner to Allah, and the other is to do harm to Muslims. — Muhammad (*s*)

It is incumbent upon my community that they associate with scholars and adhere to their advice. Surely, Allah resuscitates a dead heart with their wisdom as He revives a dry land with rain (from the sky). — Muhammad (*s*)

The person who enters the grave without doing good deeds is like a person who tries to cross a sea without a ship. — Abu Bakr as-Siddiq,[1] *radiya Allahu 'anhu* (may Allah be pleased with him).

※※※

Worldly fame is gained through wealth. Honor in the Next World is gained through good deeds. — 'Umar (r)[2]

※※※

Worldly engagements bring darkness in one's heart. Thoughts of the Hereafter bring light into

---

1. Abu Bakr Siddiq (r), a close companion of the Prophet, was born 50 before Hijrah. He was the first free adult male to convert to Islam. He became the first Caliph after the death of the Prophet. He died in Madinah at the age of 63 in 13 after Hijrah (AH). His grave lies next to that of the Prophet in Madinah.

2. 'Umar, born in 40 BH, embraced Islam in the sixth year of Prophethood and became a close companion of the Prophet. He became the second Caliph after the death of Abu Bakr. During his reign, Jerusalem, Egypt, Iraq and Persia were brought under the Islamic rule. He was the first who was given the title of Amir al-Mu'minin (Prince of the Faithful). He was assassinated by a Christian while performing the dawn (*fajr*) prayer in 23 AH. He is buried in Madinah beside the Prophet's grave.

The Counsel

one's heart. — 'Uthman[3] (*r*)

❀❀❀❀

He who seeks enlightenment is sought by Paradise. He who seeks iniquity is sought by Hell. — 'Ali (*r*)[4]

❀❀❀❀

No noble man disobeys Allah. And no wise man prefers this world (lit. *dunya*) to the Next World (lit. *akhirah*). — Yahya bin Mu'adh (*r*)[5]

---

3. 'Uthman was the third Caliph in Islam. He had the honor of marrying two daughters of the Prophet, one after the death of the other. The last years of his regime were troubled by internal dispute and riot which resulted in his assassination in 35 AH. He was 82 years old when he died. He was buried near the Jannatul Baqi in Madinah.

4. 'Ali was the cousin and son-in-law of the Prophet. He was reared by the Prophet and embraced Islam when he was only ten years old. He became the fourth Caliph in Islam after the murder of 'Uthman by rioters. His regime was marked by internal dispute. He was fatally injured by a member of the Khawarij (those who left his camp after the battle of Siffin) in 40 AH. He was then 63 years old. His mausoleum is in Najaf, Iraq. He was a vast ocean of knowledge. The Prophet said, "I am the city of knowledge, and 'Ali is its gate." His maxims are well-known in the Arabic language.

5. Yahya bin Mu'adh al-Razi, also known as Abu Zakariyya, was a native of Rayy. He was a disciple of Ibn Karram, left his native town to live for a while in Balkh, afterwards proceeding to Nishapur where he lived until his death n 258 AH. He was the author of many books and fine sayings.

There is hope for forgiveness of sins committed due to lust (lit. *shahwah*), but not so for sins committed due to pride. Allah did not forgive Satan as the root of his sin was his pride while He forgave Adam (*'alayhissalam*) as the root of his sin was his lust. — Sufyan al-Thawri (r)[6]

A saintly man said, "Allah will throw that person to hell who is gleeful of committing sinful deeds; there he or she will cry. On the other hand, Allah will enter that person to heaven who worships and cries (in fear of Him); there he or she will be joyful."

People always held him in respect.

6. Sufyan al-Thawri was born in 97 AH at Kufa and studied first under his father, and later with many learned men, especially Hisham bin 'Urwah, attaining high proficiency as a traditionist and theologian in Islam. He was a contemporary of the Imam, Abu Hanifah (r). He was persecuted by the 'Abbasid rulers for refusing to accept government office. He died in 161 AH at Basra (in southern Iraq).

A wise man said, "Never consider a minor sin to be negligible. Surely, minor sins aggregate to major sins."

When minor sins are repeatedly committed, they do not remain minor any longer. And if one continuously seeks forgiveness, his major sins do not remain major any longer. — Muhammad (*s*)

It is related that the gnostics (lit. *'arif*) are always preoccupied with meditation while the ascetics (lit. *zahid*) with supplications to Allah. This is due to the fact that a gnostic seeks his Lord only (and is, therefore, unmindful of anything but Allah) while an ascetic (strives to save) himself only.

A wise man said, "A person who assumes that there is a better patron than Allah has little knowledge (lit. *ma'rifah*) about Allah; and a person who assumes that there is a worse enemy than his *nafs* (carnal self) has little knowledge about (the evils of) his *nafs*."

❁·❁·❁

Someone said, "Lust turns a king into a slave, and self-control or steadfastness (lit. *sabr*) elevates a slave to kingship. The story of Yusuf (*a.s.*) [7] and Zulaykha[8] is a sufficient proof of this."

❁·❁·❁

Someone said, "Blessed is he who is ruled by his *'aql* (wisdom) and enslaves his *hawa'* (passion). Wretched is he who is ruled by his *hawa'* and enslaves his *'aql*."

❁·❁·❁

---

7. Prophet Joseph, son of Jacob, of the Hebrew Bible.

8. Zulaykha was the wife of a city administrator in Egypt who fell in love with Yusuf (*a.s.*). Her infatuation was so great that she wanted to seduce Yusuf (*a.s.*), but he turned her down. The story is mentioned in the twelfth chapter of the Qur'an (Surah Yusuf).

A wise man said, "He who shuns sinful deeds, his heart is softened; and he who earns a *halal* (lawful) livelihood after discarding that which is *haram* (unlawful), he attains clarity in meditation (lit. *fikr*). Allah revealed to one of His Prophets: 'Obey My command and do not disobey My admonition'."

※※※※

Someone said, "A person who strives for pleasing Allah and avoids things that displease Him has attained perfection of knowledge."

※※※※

A wise man has said, "A learned scholar is a native even in a foreign land while an ignorant man is an alien in his own locality."

※※※※

Another wise man said, "He who comes near Allah through his worship remains a stranger among his people."

A wise man said, "The proof of a gnostic is in his progress in worship just as the proof of life is in the movement of the limbs."

The root of all evils is the worldly love. The root of all troubles (lit. *fitnah*) is non-payment of *ushr* (one-tenth of agricultural produce) and *zakah* (poor-due). — Muhammad (s)

A wise man said, "He who admits his mistakes is praised by all. Admission of mistakes is a sign of one's maturity."

Someone said, "He who denies Allah's bounties (with which he was blessed) is an ingrate. And he who keeps fellowship with fools is doomed."

3

He who complains at dawn about his worldly needs actually complains against his Lord. He who is depressed with worldly affairs is actually depressed with Allah. He who is humble to some rich man on account of the latter's wealth has lost two-thirds of his religion. — Muhammad (s)

There are three things that cannot be acquired by three other things: wealth is not gained solely by desires; youth is not regained by darkening one's hair; and health is not restored by medicine alone. — Abu Bakr as-Siddiq

Half of one's intelligence lies in his keeping good relationship with others. Half of one's learning lies in his asking questions. Half of one's livelihood lies in good management of his family. — 'Umar

❧❧❧

The person who shuns the world for the love of Allah becomes His beloved. The person who avoids committing sin for fear of Allah becomes beloved of angels. The person who shuns all kinds of greed and desires from fellow Muslims is loved by them. — 'Uthman

❧❧❧

Among all the blessings in this world, surely the blessing of Islam is sufficient for you. Among all your duties and business affairs, surely the worship of Allah is a sufficient duty and business for you. Among all the lessons, surely the death of other human beings is a sufficient lesson for you. — 'Ali

❧❧❧

There are many people who rush toward sinful deeds because of the blessings of life. There are many people who are spoiled by people's adoration. There are still others who are misled by (the notion of) safety from Allah (and thus, neglect to repent in time). — 'Abdullah bin Mas'ud (r)[9]

It is revealed in the Psalms (lit. *Zabur*) that an intelligent man should not busy himself except in three matters: (1) earning provision for the Hereafter, (2) earning his livelihood and (3) seeking comfort of this world through lawful means. — Dawud (a.s.) [10], the prophet.

---

9. 'Abdullah bin Mas'ud, also known as Ibn 'Umm 'Abd, was the sixth Muslim to embrace Islam, and became one of the closest Companions of the Prophet. He was the first one to recite the Qur'an publicly in Makkah after the Prophet . He became the most learned of the *ummah* and the best one to learn the Qur'an by heart. 'Umar appointed him the Treasurer and Chief Judge of Kufa. He was the founder of the Kufan school of learning which later produced great scholars of Islam. He was very strict in matter of Prophetic narrations and used to warn his pupils against carelessness in preserving the words intact. He lived a very austere life. He died in 32 AH at the age of 60 and was buried at Jannatul Baqi in Madinah.

10. Dawud (a.s.) is the Biblical prophet, King David, the father of King Solomon.

AL-MUNABBIHAT

There are three things which protect a person; three things which ruin a person; three things which enhance one's prestige; and three things, which compensate for one's sin. The things that protect are: (1) Fear of Allah in secret and in open; (2) seeking moderation in states of poverty and riches; and (3) doing justice both in pleasure and displeasure. The three habits that ruin a person are: (1) extreme miserliness; (2) following one's passion; and (3) self-esteem or considering oneself to be better than others. The three habits which enhance one's prestige are: (1) greeting people, both known and unknown, with salutations (lit. *salam*); (2) feeding people; and (3) praying when people are asleep at night. The three habits which compensate for one's sin are: (1) making a complete *wudu'* (ritual purification) even when it is too cold; (2) walking to the place of *jama'ah* (congregational prayer); and (3) waiting after one prayer for the next prayer. — Muhammad (s), narrated by Abu Hurayrah (r)[11]

---

11. Abu Hurayrah was a Companion of the Prophet (s). He embraced Islam in 7 AH and stayed in the company of the Prophet until the latter died. He reported many *ahadith* (Prophetic traditions) which are recorded in the books of Hadith. More than 800 men narrated *ahadith* from him. He was appointed a *mufti* (scholar of Islamic verdicts) during

The Counsel

Once Gabriel (a.s.)[12] told the Prophet (s), "O Muhammad, live as long as you want but one day you have to die. You can love anyone you desire, but one day you would be separated from your lover. You can do whatever you like, but one day you have to face its consequence."

Allah will provide shade under His Throne to three kinds of people on the Day of Judgment and on that Day there will be no other shade available. These are: (1) those people who make ablution with water even if it is difficult for them, (2) those who walk to mosque even if it is dark outside, and (3) those who feed the hungry. — Muhammad (s)

Once someone asked Ibrahim (a.s.)[13], "What

---

the caliphate of 'Umar, and later became governor during the reign of Marwan bin al-Hakam. He died at the age of seventy-eight in 58 (or 59) AH and was buried at Jannatul Baqi in Madinah.

12. Gabriel (Jibril) is the angel of revelation who transmitted the Qur'an to Prophet Muhammad (s) over a period of 23 years.

13. Patriarch Abraham, the Biblical prophet.

caused to you to earn the title of *Khalil Allah* (Friend of Allah)?" He replied, "I have earned the title for three reasons. (1) I always preferred the commands of Allah over everything else, (2) I did not worry myself with things for which Allah Himself was responsible, and (3) I never took my meals in the morning and evening without entertaining guests."

A wise man said, "Three things remove man's sufferings: (1) remembrance (lit. *zikr*) of Allah, the Exalted, (2) company of friends (lit. *awliya'*) of Allah, and (3) listening to the words of wise men."

He who is devoid of manners is devoid of knowledge. He who has no patience (lit. *sabr*) has no religion (lit. *din*). He who has no piety (lit. *wara'*) is far from Allah's intimacy.

The Counsel

— Hassan al-Basri (r)[14]

❧❧❧

It is said that a man from the Children of Israel decided to go out to seek knowledge. This news reached the Prophet (s) of his time. The Prophet (s) summoned him through a messenger. When the man was brought forth, he asked him, "Son, I would like to advise you on three matters wherein lie the entire wisdom from the beginning to the end. (These are): (1) Fear Allah in all conditions, (2) avoid gossiping about others; if you, at all, need to talk about someone, only disclose his good deeds, and (3) make sure that the food you eat has come from lawful means." Upon hearing these, the man abandoned his idea of going out to search for knowledge.

❧❧❧

---

14. Hassan al-Basri, the son of a slave, was born in Madinah in 21 AH. His father became a client of the Prophet's secretary, Zaid bin Thabit. Brought up in Basrah, he had the privilege of meeting many Companions of the Prophet, including 70 of those who fought at the Battle of Badr. He grew up to become one of the most prominent personalities in Islam, being famous for his discourses, piety and austerity. He is considered to be one of the greatest saints of Islam. He died in Basrah in 110 AH.

In another narration it is said that a man from the Children of Israel acquired much knowledge from books that would fill up eighty vaults. But that knowledge was of no benefit to him. Allah, the Exalted, revealed to the prophet of that time to tell that person, "Even if you were to study more books to further your knowledge that would still be of no benefit to you as long as you do not act upon three things: (1) do not fall in love with this world for this world is not the permanent abode for the faithful believers (lit. *mu'minin*), (2) do not befriend Satan for he is not a friend of the faithful believers, and (3) do not trouble any of Allah's creation because such is not the nature of any faithful believer.

※※※※

Someone said, "That person is the most lucky of all human beings whose heart (lit. *qalb*) is full of knowledge, whose body is capable of bearing patiently, and who is satisfied with whatever (little) he/she possesses."

The Counsel

※※※※

Surely those who perished before you had three bad habits: (1) vain talks, (2) gluttony, and (3) excessive sleep. — Ibrahim al-Nakha'i (r)[15]

※※※※

That person is blessed: (1) who discards the world before the latter discards him; (2) who has acquired the provisions for protecting himself in the grave before he enters the grave; and (3) who has earned Allah's pleasure before meeting Him. — Yahya Mu'adh Razi (r)[16]

※※※※

'Ali said, "He who is devoid of *sunnah* (mode operandi or custom) of Allah, His Messenger and His intimate friends (lit. *awliya'*) is devoid of

---

15. Ibrahim al-Nakha'i was a Successor, who met several Companions of the Prophet (s). He was a famous scholar in exegesis of the Qur'an and was a teacher of Hammad, the teacher of Imam Abu Hanifah. He was well-known for his piety and truthfulness. He died in 95 AH.

16. Same as Yahya bin Mu'adh al-Razi.

everything." He was asked, "What is the *sunnah* of Allah?" He replied, "It is to hide the shortcomings and secrets of people." He was next asked, "What is the *sunnah* of the Prophet?" He replied, "Good manners with people." He was then asked, "What is the *sunnah* of *awliya'*?" He replied, "It is to endure patiently the bad manners of people."

※※※

The sages of the past used to advise people with three things and would have these written down: (1) He who works for the Next World, Allah will take care of his affairs both in this world and the next. (2) He who reforms his inner state, Allah will reform his outer state, too. (3) He who amends the affairs between himself and Allah, Allah will straighten the affairs between him and other human beings.

※※※

Be the best man to Allah, the worst man to your carnal self (lit. *nafs*) and a layman among the masses. — 'Ali

The Counsel

Allah revealed to 'Uzayr (*a.s.*)[17] the prophet: "When you commit even a small sin, do not overlook such, but be terrified that you have violated Allah's command. When you are blessed with something little, do not be concerned about its pettiness, but be mindful of Who has blessed you. When you run into any difficulty, do not complain against Me to others, just as I do not speak ill of you to the angels who inform Me about your evil deeds."

Every morning Satan asks me three questions: "(1) what will you eat, (2) what will you wear, and (3) where will you live today?" In reply I tell him: "(1) I shall eat death, (2) wear the burial shroud, and (3) live in the grave." — Hatim al-Assam (*r*)[18]

---

17. Same as Ezra the scribe in the Jewish Bible.

18. Abu 'Abd ar-Rahman Hatim al-Assam was a native of Balkh (Afghanistan). He was a pupil of Shaqiq al-Balkhi, another great saint of Islam. He was a very charitable man and it is said that he never lied in his life. He has many lofty sayings. He is the author of famous works on ethics (*'ilm al-mu'amalat*). He died near Tirmiz (in present day Afghanistan) in 237 AH.

He who approaches Allah from disobedience to obedience, Allah makes him wealthy without wealth, strong without soldiers and honorable without being raised in a noble family.
— Muhammad (s)

Once the Messenger of Allah (s) approached his Companions and asked them, "In what condition did you find yourself this morning?" They replied, "We got up with *iman* (faith) in Allah." He asked, "What is the sign of your *iman*?" They replied, "(1) When in trouble, we patiently endure. (2) We thank Allah when in peace and happiness. (3) We are content with Allah's decree." Then the Messenger of Allah (s) said, "I testify by the Lord of the Ka'bah that all of you are true believers (lit. *mu'minin*)."

It is narrated that Allah revealed to a prophet

The Counsel

(*a.s.*): (1) He who meets Me with fondness, I grant him Paradise. (2) He who is scared of meeting Me, I keep him away from Hell. (3) He who meets Me with modesty, I make the record-keeping angels heedless of his sins."

ಸಿ.ಸಿ.ಸಿ.

Fulfill your obligations to Allah and you will become the best worshipper or devotee among men. Avoid all the forbidden things that Allah has decreed and you will become the most ascetic of all. Be pleased with what Allah has decreed for you and you will become the richest of all. — 'Abdullah bin Mas'ud

ಸಿ.ಸಿ.ಸಿ.

While he was passing by some houses, Salih Marqadi (*r*)[19] questioned, "O the dwelling places! Where did your former masters perish? Where are your original builders? And where are your past dwellers?" At that time he heard a supernatural

---

19. Salih Marqadi was a Muslim saint.

voice saying, "All their signs have perished. The earth has decomposed their body. And only their deeds are hanging (now) like necklaces."

※※※※

You help anyone and you are his master. You beg from anyone and you are his captive for life. Instead of depending on anyone, if you decide to remain self-reliant then you will be his equal.
— 'Ali

※※※※

Someone asked Ibrahim bin Adham (r),[20] "How were you able to cut your ties to this world?" He replied, "I have been able to do so because of three things: (1) I recognized the grave to be the most dreadful place to live, yet there will not be any companion therein to help me. (2) I realized that my journey was a long and a tortuous one, yet I did not have the necessary provisions to partake in

---

20. Ibrahim bin Adham was born in Balkh (Afghanistan) in a princely family, who renounced his kingdom to live a life of complete asceticism. He died around 165 AH. He was a disciple of Imam Abu Hanifah.

that journey. (3) I realized that the Lord of the Day of Judgment was Allah, the Most Powerful, yet I did not have the necessary deeds for my salvation."

※※※※

Someone asked Sufyan al-Thawri, "What is the meaning of love for Allah?" He replied, "It means not to be captivated by any beautiful face, melodious voice and eloquent speech."

※※※※

The word *zuhd* (ascetic detachment) is comprised of three Arabic letters: *za*, *ha* and *dal*. *Za* stands for increasing (lit. *zadun*) provisions for the Next World, *ha* stands for seeking guidance (lit. *huda*) in religious affairs (lit. *din*) and *dal* stands for remaining constantly consumed (lit. *dawamun*) in obedience (lit. *ta'ah*) of Allah. — Ibn 'Abbas (r)[21]

---

21. 'Abdullah bin 'Abbas was the cousin of the Prophet (s). He was only three years old when the Prophet (s) migrated from Makkah to Madinah. He was an advisor to 'Ali during the civil war. He was a great commentator of the Qur'an and is credited with the establishment of the Makkan school of learning. He died at Ta'if in 68 AH.

The word *zuhd* (ascetic detachment) is comprised of three Arabic letters. The letter *za* stands for shunning worldly charms (lit. *zinat*), *ha* stands for shunning carnal desires (lit. *hawa'*) and *dal* stands for discarding this world (lit. *dunya*). — Ibn 'Abbas

It is narrated from Hamid Lafaf (*r*)[22] that a man asked him, "Counsel me." He said, "Put on a wrapper of religion just as there is a wrapping cloth for the Qur'an." Someone then asked him, "What is the wrapper of religion?" He replied, "It means not to speak unless it is absolutely necessary, to discard worldly things that are superfluous and to avoid association with worldly people unless it is necessary."

---

22. Hamid Lafaf was a Muslim divine.

The Counsel

Luqman Hakim (*r*)[23] once advised his son, "O my dear son, there are three parts to a human being: *ruh* (spirit), *nafs* (soul) and body (of flesh and blood). The *ruh* is for Allah, the *nafs* is for your deeds, and your body is for the insects."

※※※

Three things increase one's memory and protect one against coughing. These are: (1) brushing the teeth with a tooth-stick, (2) fasting, and (3) reciting the Qur'an. — 'Ali

※※※

There are three fortresses for believers against Satan. These are: (1) mosque, (2) remembrance of Allah and (3) recitation of the Qur'an. — Ka'b al-Ahbar (*r*)[24]

---

23. Luqman Hakim or Luqman the Sage was a pre-Islamic wise man who is mentioned in the Qur'an (see Surah Luqman). It is widely believed that he lived in Africa. He is credited with many maxims.

24. Ka'b al-Ahbar (lit. "Ka'b the Hebrew") was a learned Jewish rabbi, born into a Jewish scholarly family from Yemen, who converted to Islam and contributed greatly to the commentary of the Israeli traditions in the Qur'an. He died around 652 AD.

A wise man once said, "There are three things which are preserved in the treasury of Allah. He grants these to only those whom He loves. These three things are: (1) poverty, (2) disease and (3) patience."

Someone once asked Ibn 'Abbas, "Among all the days what is the best day?" He replied, "The day of Jum'ah (i.e., Friday)." He was again asked, "What is the best month?" He replied, "The month of Ramadan." He was then asked, "What is the best deed (lit. *'amal*)?" He replied, "To establish the five daily prayers at the appointed hours." After three days, when 'Ali was informed of Ibn 'Abbas's answers to those questions, he remarked, "If all the scholars, sages and jurists from the East to the West were asked of those questions, they could not have answered in a better way. But let me state that the best deed is the one that is accepted by Allah. The best month is that month in which you returned to Allah after repenting for your sins. And

The Counsel

the best day is that day in which you leave this world to meet Allah, the Exalted, with your faith intact."

꒰꒰꒰

It is related (from Hadith), "If Allah wishes to do good to someone, He endows that person with the knowledge of religion, the strength to discard worldly comforts and the eyes to see his own errors."

꒰꒰꒰

It is reported that Muhammad (s) once said, "Three things of this world are dear to me. These are: (1) perfume, (2) women (wives) and (3) prayer—the comfort of my eyes." In that gathering his Companions were also present. (Among them) Abu Bakr as-Siddiq said, "O Messenger of Allah, you have spoken the truth. There are three things of this world which are dear to me. These are: (1) To gaze at the holy face of the Messenger of Allah, (2) to spend my wealth for the sake of the Messenger of Allah, and (3) the privilege of having my daughter married to the Messenger of Allah." Then 'Umar said, "O Abu Bakr, you have spoken the truth. There are also three things of this world that are dear to me. These are: (1) to encourage people to do good deeds, (2) to discourage people from doing bad deeds and (3) to be clothed in old garments." Next 'Uthman said, "O 'Umar, you have spoken the truth. There are three things of this world which are dear to me. These are: (1) To feed the hungry, (2) to clothe the unclad, and (3) to recite the Qur'an." Then 'Ali said, "O 'Uthman, you have spoken the truth. There are three things of this world that are also dear to me. These are: (1) to serve guests, (2) to fast during hot summer months, and (3) to take arms against the unbelievers." During their discussion, Jibril (*a.s.*) appeared there and informed them, "Allah heard what you have said and sent me forth in order that you (Muhammad) may inquire of me as to what things of this world would I have liked if I were its inhabitant." Then Muhammad (*s*) asked him, "If you were an inhabitant of this world, what are the things you would have liked?" Jibril (*a.s.*) replied, "If I had been like you, I would have loved three things: (1) guide those who are misled, (2) love the indigent who are devoted to prayers and (3) help those poor men who look after large families." He continued, "Allah likes three things in His slaves. These are: (1) to strive in the path of Allah with vigor, (2) to shed tears in repentance of sins committed, and (3) to endure hardship (lit. *faqah*) patiently."

A wise man said, "(1) Those who only rely on their own reasoning (in all matters) will be misled. (2) Those who become haughty on account of wealth will be demeaned. And (3) those who seek honor and prestige due to creation will be disgraced."

A wise man said, "There are three qualities which are the roots of *ma'rifah* (gnosis). These are: (1) remaining always bashful in the presence of Allah, (2) loving someone or something for the sake of Allah, and (3) maintaining fellowship with Allah."

True love resides in three habits: (1) preferring one's friend over others in speech or advice, (2) preferring the company of one's friend over others, and (3) preferring one's friend over others in satisfying his needs. — Muhammad (s)

※※※

It is written in the Tawrah (Torah): (1) The avaricious man is always needy, even when he becomes the king of the world. (2) Everyone will follow those who follow Allah's commandments, even though he may be a slave (of someone else). (3) He is indeed rich who is satisfied with little, even though he may be starving. — Wahb bin Munabbih (r)[25]

※※※

---

25. Wahb bin Munabbih, like Ka'b al-Ahbar, was a convert to Islam. He was a Yemenite and a Successor (*tabi'i*) to the Companions. His mother claimed descent from the Himyarite kings of South Yemen; his father was of Persian descent, sent to Yemen as a soldier by the Persian emperor Khushraw Anushirwan. He was an authority on the ancient traditions of Arabia and the People of the Book, Jews and Christians. He contributed greatly to Muslim understanding of Jewish traditions in the Qur'an. He died at San'a, Yemen, in 110 AH/728 AD during the early days of the caliphate of Hisham bin 'Abd al-Malik.

The Counsel

A wise man said, "(1) The *'arif* (gnostic) of Allah does not befriend *makhluq* (the created objects). (2) Those who know the real value of this world do not have any attachment to it. (3) Those who are aware of Allah's Judgment do not entertain any grudge against any of their worst enemies."

☙❧☙❧

He who is afraid is a fugitive. He who is eager is a seeker. He who is a lover of Allah is afraid (of the evils) of his *nafs* (carnal self). — Dhu al-Nun al-Misri (r)[26]

☙❧☙❧

Gnostics are prisoners in this world. Their hearts can see. Their virtuous deeds in the path of Allah are plentiful. — Dhu al-Nun al-Misri

---

[26]. Dhu al-Nun al-Misri was the son of a Nubian and born in Upper Egypt around 180 AH. He studied under various teachers and traveled extensively. He was a spiritual king, who is credited with many miracles, and famed for his penances, austerities and worship. He died in Cairo in 246 AH.

AL-MUNABBIHAT

Only the gnostics are obedient to Allah. Their hearts are pure. Their deeds in the path of Allah are spotless. — Dhu al-Nun al-Misri

(1) The root of all virtuous deeds in this world and the next is the fear of Allah. (2) The key to all bad deeds in this world is gluttony. And (3) the key to attaining a blessed state in the Next World is hunger. — Ibn Sulayman al-Darani (r)[27]

Someone said, "*Ibadah* (worship) is like a profession: its work place is seclusion. Its capital is *taqwa* (fear of Allah). And its profit is *jannah* (Paradise)."

---

27. The Arabic manuscript mentions Ibn and not Abu Sulayman al-Darani, who is unknown to this compiler. However, if it is assumed that there was a copying error in the manuscript, then the latter personality is well known. Abu Sulayman was held in high honor by the Sufis. He is distinguished by his severe austerities and acts of self-mortification (see *Kashf al-Mahjub*).

The Counsel

Rid yourself of three bad habits with three good ones in order that you can be considered a true believer: (1) Pride with humility, (2) greed with contentment in little, and (3) envy (lit. *hasad*) with good advice. — Malik bin Dinar (r)[28]

---

28. Malik bin Dinar al-Sami was the son of a slave from Sijistan, near Kabul (in Afghanistan) and studied under Hassan al-Basri and Muhammad bin Sirin. He was a reliable traditionist who transmitted from such early authorities as Anas bin Malik and Ibn Sirin. He was also an early calligrapher of the Qur'an. He lived a very pious and ascetic life, and was noted for performing many miracles. He died around 130 AH.

4

It is narrated from Abu Dharr al-Ghifari (*r.a.*)[29] that Muhammad (*s*) said, "O Abu Dharr, strengthen your sailboat (of faith), because the sea (of faith) is too deep. Gather enough provision for the trip is too long. Lighten the burden of your sin for the destination is arduous. Be sincere in your deeds for the scrutinizer is discerning."

※※※※

An Arab poet wrote,
 "Repentance (from sin) is obligatory for all men but to avoid sin is better.

---

29. Abu Dharr al-Ghifari, an early convert to Islam, was a close Companion of the Prophet (*s*). He was a devoted ascetic who lived a monastic life. He was opposed to capitalism and materialism, and never shied away from speaking the truth. He lived in Madina during the Caliphate of the first two caliphs, and then moved to Syria during the Caliphate of 'Uthman. There he came in conflict with Mu'awiyah, the governor of Syria, and was called back to return to Madina. He settled at Rabdhah, outside Madinah, where he died in 32 AH. 'Abdullah bin Mas'ud led his funeral prayer.

The Counsel

Patience in calamity is difficult,
But to be deprived of its reward (being impatient) is a greater calamity.
The evolution of time is amazing,
But more amazing is the indolence of human beings.
Every newcomer is nearby but death is nearer."

⁂

A wise man said, "Four deeds are good. But these are even better depending on the time and the people involved. (These are:) (1) Shyness (or modesty) in man is good but is better in woman. (2) Doing justice is good for all but is better for the rulers and leaders. (3) Repentance is good for the elderly but is better for young men. (4) Generosity is good for the affluent but is better for the indigent."

⁂

A wise man said, "Four deeds are bad, but these are even worse depending on the time and the people involved: (1) Committing sin is bad for young men but is worse for the elderly. (2) Engagement in worldly affairs is bad for laymen but is worse for the learned. (3) Laziness in worship is bad for all but is worse for both teachers and students. (4) Pride is bad for the wealthy but is worse for the indigent."

❧❦❧

The planets in the sky are shields for the dwellers in heaven, but what a disaster will that be when these will be scattered. The members of my family are the shields for my community but what a disaster will that be when they will not be there. I am a shield for my Companions but what a disaster that will be when I will depart from them. The mountains are like shields that protect the inhabitants of this earth but what a disaster will that be when these will disintegrate.
— Muhammad (s)

❧❦❧

There are four things that are consummated by

The Counsel

four others. These are: (1) Errors in *salah* (prayer) by two additional acts of prostration, (2) fasting (in the month of Ramadan) by paying *fitrah* (a fixed amount of charity), (3) hajj (pilgrimage) by sacrificing an animal, and (4) faith by (participating in) *jihad* (striving in the path of Allah). — Abu Bakr as-Siddiq

❁❁❁❁

(1) Whoever establishes twelve units (lit. *rak'ah*) of prayer daily (besides the five daily *fard* or compulsory prayers) has discharged the rights of prayer. (2) Whoever fasts three days in a month has discharged the rights of fasting. (3) Whoever recites one hundred verses from the Qur'an daily has discharged the rights of the recitation (of the Qur'an). (4) Whoever donates a *dirham* on (every) Friday has discharged the rights of charity.
— 'Abdullah bin Mubarak (*r*)[30]

---

30. 'Abdullah bin Mubarak was a disciple of Imam Abu Hanifah and Imam Malik bin Anas. He was born in 118 AH. He traveled extensively collecting Prophetic traditions and became a reliable authority on Hadith. He was noted for his opposition to heresy and criticism of unreliable traditions. He became an ascetic and distributed his wealth among the poor. He died in 181 AH.

There are four types of ocean: (1) passion (lit. *hawa'*) is the ocean of sin (lit. *zunub*); (2) the carnal soul (lit. *nafs*) is the ocean of lust (lit. *shahwah*); (3) death (lit. *mawt*) is the ocean of extinction of life (lit. *a'mar*); and (4) grave (lit. *qabr*) is the ocean of distress or contrition (lit. *nadamah*). — 'Umar

I have found the sweetness of worship in four things. (1) The first of these was fulfilling the obligatory duties due to Allah. (2) The second was to avoid those things that were forbidden by Him. (3) The third was to exhort people to good deeds, hoping for His reward. (4) And the fourth was to admonish people from doing evil, fearing His wrath. — 'Uthman

There are four things that are outwardly blessings but are inwardly obligatory: (1) Company of the righteous people is a blessing, but following them is an obligation. (2) Recitation of the Qur'an is a blessing, but acting on its instructions is an obligation. (3) Visiting the graveyard is a blessing, but earning its provisions is obligatory. (4) Caring for the sick is a blessing, but taking lessons from it (sickness) is obligatory. — 'Uthman

(1) Those who aspire for the Paradise do good deeds. (2) Those afraid of the Hell Fire enslave lust. (3) Those sure about death are bitter about this world. (4) Those who know the world will have their troubles taken care of. — 'Ali

(1) Prayer is the pillar of religion, but silence (or avoiding vain talks) is better. (2) Sadaqah (alms-giving) cools down my Lord's wrath, but silence is better. (3) Fasting is a curtain against the Hell Fire, but silence is better. (4) *Jihad* (striving) glorifies religion, but silence is better.
— Muhammad (s)

It is narrated that Allah, the Exalted, revealed to a prophet among the Children of Israel: "(1) When you safeguard your tongue from vile talks, it is like a fasting for Me. (2) When you safeguard your limbs from committing *haram* (prohibited) things, it is like a prayer for Me. (3) When you safeguard yourself from seeking aid from creation, it is like a charity for Me. (4) When you safeguard the believers from oppression, it is like a *jihad* (holy war) for Me."

Four things darken the heart: (1) gluttony, (2) the company of oppressive people, (3) obliviousness of past sins, and (4) high aspirations. Four other things illuminate one's heart: (1) an empty stomach (i.e., living in hunger for fear of committing sin), (2) the company of righteous people, (3) recognition of one's past sins, and (4) curtailed desires. — 'Abdullah bin Mas'ud

The Counsel

(1) He who claims to love Allah but does not avoid things forbidden by Allah is a liar. (2) He who claims to love the Prophet but does not care for the poor is a liar. (3) He who claims to love Paradise but is not charitable is a liar. (4) He who claims to fear the Fire (Hell) but does not avoid sinful acts is a liar. — Hatim Assam

❁❁❁

The signs of man's misfortune are four. These are: (1) to forget about past sins while those are all preserved with Allah, the Exalted, (2) to reminisce about past virtuous deeds while he is not aware whether such were accepted (as good deeds) or not, (3) to look at those who are richer than him, and (4) to esteem himself to be religiously better by looking at someone who is inferior to him. Allah says about these kinds of people, "I desired to favor them but they rejected My favor." (On the other hand) the signs of fortune are also four. These are: (1) to reminisce about past sins, (2) to overlook one's past virtuous deeds, (3) to look at those who are more pious than he is and (4) to compare himself with those who are financially worse off than he is. — Muhammad (s)

༺༻

A wise man said, "There are four signs of a man's *iman* (faith): (1) *taqwa* (fear of God), (2) *haya'* (shyness), (3) *shukr* (thankfulness), and (4) *sabr* (patience and steadfastness)."

༺༻

(1) Eating less is the mother of all medicines (*ummul 'adwiyah*). (2) Speaking less is the mother of good manners (*ummul adab*). (3) Avoiding sinful acts is the mother of worship (*ummul 'ibadah*). (4) Patience (*sabr*) is the mother of high aspirations (*ummul amani*). — Muhammad (s)

༺༻

There are four precious elements with man—*'aql, din, haya'* and *'amal al-salih*—which are ravaged by four other items. For example: (1) *'aql* (wisdom) ravaged by *ghadab* (anger); (2) *din* (religion)

ravaged by *hasad* (envy); (3) *haya'* (modesty and shyness) ravaged by *tama'* (greed or high aspirations); (4) *'amal al-salih* (virtuous deeds) ravaged by *ghibah* (backbiting and slandering).
— Muhammad (s)

There are four heavenly things that are better than Paradise itself. (1) The eternal life in Paradise is better than Paradise itself. (2) The service of angels in Paradise is better than Paradise itself. (3) The company of the prophets in Paradise is better than Paradise itself. (4) Earning the pleasure of Allah is better than Paradise itself.
— Muhammad (s)

There are four things in Hell that are worse than Hell itself. (These are:) (1) Eternal life in Hell is worse than Hell itself. (2) The insolent condemnation of the unbelievers by the angels in Hell is worse than Hell itself. (3) The company of Satan in Hell is worse than Hell itself. (4) Earning

the wrath of Allah is worse than Hell itself.
— Muhammad (s)

⁂

A wise man said, "Whenever people ask me on my condition, I tell them that (1) I am in agreement with (the decrees of) my Lord, (2) I am engaged in warfare against my *nafs* (carnal self), (3) I am engaged in enjoining good advice to people, and (4) I am engaged with the *dunya* (world) only to the barest necessity (for survival)."

⁂

A wise man gathered four precious sayings from the Scriptures. (1) From the Tawrah (Torah): He who is content with what has been allotted to him by Allah, the Exalted, will lead a comfortable life both in this world and the next. (2) From the Injil (Gospel): He who bridles his carnal desires will be honored both in this world and the next. (3) From the Zabur (Psalms): He who secludes himself by giving up unnecessary association with people will be saved both in this world and the next. (4) From the Qur'an: He who safeguards his tongue from vain talks will be in peace both in this world and the next.

❧❧❧

I swear by Allah that whenever I endured any hardship, I have always been blessed with four bounties from Allah, the Exalted. The first is that when that hardship was not caused by my sin (I will get reward for that). The second is that when that hardship was not worse than my sin (I will get reward for that). The third is that I am not deprived of contentment (since that hardship occurred according to Allah's decree). The fourth is that I hope for reward from Allah by enduring the hardship. — 'Umar

❧❧❧

A wise man collected many *ahadith*. Out of this he selected forty thousand *ahadith*. Next, out of those he selected four thousand *ahadith*. Next, out of those he selected four hundred *ahadith*. Out of those he then selected forty *ahadith*. At last, out of those forty he selected only four as the most important admonitions. These are: (1) do not ever depend upon women, (2) do not be deceived by your wealth, (3) do not overburden your stomach with something which it cannot digest, and (4) do not seek that knowledge which is of no benefit to you." — 'Abdullah bin Mubarak

It is narrated that Muhammad bin Ahmad explained the Qur'anic verse "... *wa sayyidan wa hasuran wa nabiyan min al-salihin*" (meaning: lordly, chaste and a Prophet of the righteous) as, "Allah, the Honored and the Glorified, referred to Yahya (i.e., John the Baptist) as *Sayyid* or lordly despite the fact that he was nothing more than His slave. This is due to the fact that he was triumphant over four things: (1) his carnal desire, (2) Iblis (the accursed Satan), (3) his tongue and (4) his anger."

This world and the *din* (religion) will remain intact

as long as there are four things. These are: (1) The rich in the society are not miserly in their spending in the path of Allah. (2) The learned men (of religion) follow the teachings. (3) The ignorant men do not boast of their knowledge in matters on which they know very little of. (4) The poor in the society do not sell the Next World in lieu of this world. — 'Ali

On the Day of Judgment, surely Allah, the Exalted, will bring four human beings as proofs against four classes of people. (1) Sulayman bin Dawud (*a.s.*) (King Solomon, the son of King David) against the rich, (2) Yusuf (*a.s.*) (Joseph, the son of Jacob) against the slaves or servants, (3) Ayyub (*a.s.*) (Job) against the sick, and (4) 'Isa (*a.s.*) (Jesus, the son of Mary) against the poor.
— Muhammad (*s*)

Even when a person commits sinful deeds Allah does not terminate four types of blessings on His slaves. (1) His provisions are not stopped. (2) His health is not ruined. (3) His evil deeds are not disclosed. (4) He is not immediately punished (for his sin). — Sa'd bin Bilal

A person will be admitted to Paradise if he sacrifices four things for gaining four other things: (1) sleep for the grave; (2) pride (lit. *fakhr*) for the (weightiness of the Scale of) Balance (*Mizan*) (on the Day of Judgment); (3) worldly comfort for (ease of crossing) the *Sirat* (the Bridge to Paradise); (4) carnal desire for Paradise. — Hatim Assam

I mistakenly sought four things in four others but did not find them there. Later I found them in four other things. (1) I sought richness (lit. *ghina*) in wealth (lit. *mal*), but found it in contentment (lit. *qana'ah*). (2) I sought comfort (lit. *rahah*) in much wealth (lit. *tharwah*), but found it in less wealth. (3) I sought pleasure (lit. *lazzah*) in bounties (of

this world), but found it in good health. (4) I sought provision (lit. *rizq*) in this earth, but found it with Allah (lit. in the heaven).
— Hamid Lafaf

There are four things, even in small quantities, whose effects are great: (1) pain, (2) poverty, (3) fire, and (4) enmity. — 'Ali

None can assess the true value of four things except four categories of people: (1) the value of youth except the old, (2) the value of comfort except the afflicted, (3) the value of health except the sick, and (4) the value of life except the dead.
— Hatim Assam

AL-MUNABBIHAT

The poet Abu Nuwas[31] wrote,
When I look at my sins I find them plenty,
But when I recount Allah's favor upon me I find it infinite.
I have no hope in my good deeds,
I only hope in Allah's mercy.
He is my Guardian, He is my Creator,
And I have entrusted myself unto Him as one who is weak and frail.
If I am forgiven it is because of His Mercy,
And if I am not forgiven, what can I do, what will be my fate?

---

31. Abu Nuwas al-Hassan Ibn Hani al-Hakami was born in 747 or 762 AD in Ahvaz, Persia and died around 813 AD in Baghdad. He was an important poet of the early 'Abbasid period (750-835 AD). Abu Nuwas, of mixed Arab and Persian heritage, studied in Basrah and Kufah, first under the poet Walibah bin al-Hubab, later under Khalaf al-Ahmar. He also studied the Qur'an (Islamic sacred scripture), Hadith (traditions relating to the life and utterances of the Prophet) and grammar, and is said to have spent a year with the Bedouins in the desert to acquire their traditional purity of language. Abu Nuwas's initial appearance at the 'Abbasid court in Baghdad met with little success; his alliance with the Barmakids, the 'Abbasid viziers, forced him to seek refuge in Egypt when the Barmakid dynasty collapsed. On his return to Baghdad, however, his panegyrics earned the favor of the caliphs Harun al-Rashid and al-Amin, and he enjoyed great success in the 'Abbasid court until his death. (*Encyclopedia Britannica*)

The Counsel

On the Day of Judgment the Measuring Balance will be set. Those who used to pray will be brought forth and they will be rewarded according to their virtuous deeds. Then those who performed the hajj will be called and they, too, will be rewarded according to their virtuous deeds. Next, those who endured hardship will be brought forth, but no measure of their virtues will be taken, nor will their book of deeds be opened. They will be rewarded so immensely for enduring their hardship that the happy ones (i.e., those granted ease and comfort in this world) will wish that had they been struck by such hardship (in the world as these enduring ones, then) they could earn the same reward from Allah, the Exalted.
— Muhammad (*s*)

❧❧❧

A wise man said, "Man encounters four types of plundering: (1) the plunder of his spirit (lit. *ruh*) by the angel of death, (2) the plunder of wealth by his heirs, (3) the plunder of his body (in the grave) by worms and insects, and (4) the plunder of his good deeds by his creditors on the Day of

Judgment (for whatever he owed to them)."

❧❦❧

A wise man said, "He who commits adultery being enslaved by lust will need women (to fulfill his lust). He who intends to become prosperous by amassing wealth will have *haram* (forbidden) earnings. He who intends to help other Muslims will have to be generous. He who intends to dedicate himself to worship (of Allah) will have to acquire knowledge."

❧❦❧

Of all deeds four are very difficult to perform: (1) forgiveness in the state of anger, (2) generosity (lit. *jud*) in the state of poverty, (3) chastity (lit. *'iffah*) while in seclusion (lit. *khalwah*), and (4) utterance of truth in front of someone who is being feared or besought (for help). — 'Ali

❧❦❧

Allah revealed to Dawud (*a.s.*) through His Book,

The Counsel

Zabur (Psalms), "An intelligent man should divide his time into four parts. One part should be dedicated to worshipping Allah. One part should be dedicated to accounting for his own deeds. One part should be dedicated to meeting those people who could show his faults (and suggest remedial measures). One part should be dedicated to earning *halal* (permissible) earnings."

☙❧☙❧

A wise man said, "The sum and substance of worship (lit. *'ibadah*) is in four things: (1) fulfilling one's vows, (2) abiding by the limits of the law (of Shari'ah), (3) persevering when something is lost, and (4) being content with whatever little one has."

5

The person who dishonors five types of people will be a loser in five matters: (1) The person who dishonors religious scholars (lit. *'ulama'*) will be a loser in (matters of) religion (lit. *din*); (2) the person who dishonors the ruler will be a loser in this world; (3) the person who harms his neighbors will lose many benefits; (4) the person who harms his relatives will be a loser through separation; (5) the person who harms his own family will be a loser by ruining happiness in his domestic life.
— Muhammad (*s*)

※※※※

In near future there will come a time when my community (lit. *ummah*) will love five things while forgetting about five other things. (1) They will love this world but forget about the Next World (lit. *akhirah*). (2) They will love their (temporal) homes but forget about graves. (3) They will love

The Counsel

wealth but forget about the accounting on the Day of Judgment. (4) They will love their families but forget about the pure companions in the heaven (lit. Hur). (5) They will love their carnal selves but forget about Allah. — Muhammad (*s*)

❁❁❁

Allah does not bestow five qualities on anyone without bestowing five other gifts. These are: (1) When a person shows gratitude (lit. *shukr*), Allah raises his dignity; (2) when a person makes *du'a* (supplication), Allah fulfills his supplication; (3) when a person begs for mercy, Allah forgives him; (4) when a person repents, Allah accepts his repentance; (5) when a person spends money in *sadaqah* (charity), Allah fulfills his request.
— Muhammad (*s*)

❁❁❁

There are five kinds of darkness (which everyone has to encounter) and these are illuminated by five kinds of lamps. (1) The love of the *dunya* is darkness and *taqwa* (fear of Allah) is its lamp. (2)

Sin is darkness and repentance is its lamp. (3) Grave is darkness and (the belief there is no god but Allah and Muhammad is His Messenger) is its lamp. (4) *Akhirah* (Hereafter) is darkness and its lamp is good deeds. (5) The *Sirat* (the Bridge on the Day of Judgment) is darkness and its lamp is *yaqin* (certainty of faith). — Abu Bakr as-Siddiq

It is related from 'Umar that either he or Muhammad (*s*) said, "If there were no fear of the claim to knowing the future, I would have testified that the following five categories of people will enter Paradise. (1) Those poor men who struggled to provide sustenance for their large families; (2) those women whose husbands were pleased with them; (3) those women who (waived the payment of or) returned dowry (lit. *mahr*) to their poor husbands; (4) those children whose parents were pleased with them; (5) those who sought forgiveness for their sins."

The Counsel

The signs of those people who fear Allah (lit. *muttaqin*) are five. (1) They only associate with those people with whom their religion remains intact. (2) They excel in subduing their modesty and tongues. (3) When they are privileged with too much bounties of this world, they consider such to be means of affliction for them (in the Next World), while when they find their minor religious deeds to have been accepted, they consider such to be exceptional. (4) They do not fill their stomachs (even) with *halal* (permitted) food fearing that anything *haram* (forbidden) might be mixed with it. (5) They consider themselves ruined while the rest of the people to have earned salvation.
— 'Uthman

❧❧❧

Every person would have been counted as a righteous person had it not been for five defects in their characters. These are: (1) apathy towards one's own ignorance, (2) worldly love, (3) miserliness even when blessed (with wealth and properties), (4) self-adulation while doing good deeds, and (5) boasting of one's own intelligence.

— 'Ali

❁❁❁❁

Those who do the following five things will be successful both in this world and the Next. (1) They do *zikr* (remembrance) of *"La ilaha illa Allah Muhammadur-Rasulullah* (there is no god but Allah and Muhammad is His Messenger)." (2) They supplicate *"inna lillahi wa inna ilayhi raji'un* (Surely we are for Allah and to Him is our return)" and *"La hawla wala quwwata illa billahil 'ali al-'azim* (There is no power or might except in Allah, the All-knowing, the Great)" when faced with hardship. (3) They thank Allah by saying, *"Alhamdulillahi Rabbil 'Alamin* (Praise be to Allah, the Lord of the Worlds)" whenever they are granted a favor. (4) They invoke Allah by saying, *"Bismillahir Rahmanir Rahim* (In the name of Allah, the Beneficent, the Merciful)" when they begin to do anything. (5) They entreat Allah by saying, *"Astagfirullah al-'azim wa a-tubu ilayh* (I seek forgiveness from Allah, the Great and I repent to you)" whenever they commit a sin. — 'Abdullah

The Counsel

bin 'Amr bin al-'As (r)[32]

❊❊❊

These five sentences are found in the Tawrah (Torah): "(1) Opulence is in contentment in little (lit. *qana'ah*), (2) peace is in solitude, (3) honor is in subduing lust, (4) fortune (from good works) is in long life and (5) patience is for short duration."
— Hassan al-Basri

❊❊❊

One should value five things in life before five other things: (1) Youth before old age, (2) health before sickness, (3) wealth before poverty, (4) life before death, and (5) leisure before work.
— Muhammad (s)

❊❊❊

---

32. 'Abdullah bin 'Amr bin al-'As was a close Companion of the Prophet (s), who embraced Islam before his father. He was a worshiping saint who fasted most of the days of his life and stood in prayer most of the night. He was a generous host and liked to feed the poor. As a great scholar of Islam, he had a great memory and was well-versed in both Arabic and Hebrew. He died at the age of 72.

(1) The person who is given to satisfying his appetite will become fleshy. (2) The person who becomes fleshy will have high carnal desires. (3) The person who has high carnal desires will commit much sin. (4) The person who commits much sin will have his heart hardened. (5) The person whose heart is hardened will drown himself into this world and its ornaments. — Yahya bin Mu'adh al-Razi

Dervishes (lit. *fuqara'*) have accepted five things and the wealthy (another) five things. The things which the dervishes accepted are: (1) peace of mind, (2) generosity of heart, (3) obedience to God, (4) easy accounting (on the Day of Judgment), and (5) exalted positions in the Next World. The things that the wealthy people accepted are: (1) restless minds, (2) busy hearts (in worldly affairs), (3) worldliness (lit. worship of the *dunya*), (4) difficult accountings (on the Day of Judgment) and (5) the lowest rankings (in the Next World). — Sufyan al-Thawri

The Counsel

The cures for the *qalb* (heart) are five: (1) the company of the righteous people, (2) the recitation of the Qur'an, (3) an empty stomach, (4) vigils at night (through worship), and (5) sincere petition for Allah's forgiveness before the daybreak.
— 'Abdullah al-Antaki (r)[33]

The scholars of Islam have said, "Inner contemplation (lit. *fikr*) is of five types. (1) Meditation on the signs of Allah—this helps one to have firm belief in monotheism and have certitude (lit. *yaqin*). (2) Meditation on the favors of Allah—this generates love for Allah. (3) Meditation on the promises of Allah—this encourages worship to Allah. (4) Meditation on the warnings of Allah—this generates fear of Him. (5) Meditation

---

33. Abu 'Abdullah Ahmad bin 'Asim al-Antaki lived to a great age and associated with the ancient Sufi *shaykhs* (teachers), and was acquainted with those who belonged to the third generation after Prophet Muhammad (s). He was a contemporary of Bishr al-Hafi and Sari al-Saqati, and a pupil of Harith al-Muhasibi, all great saints. He befriended Fudayl bin 'Iyad, another great divine, who lived during the reign of the caliph Harun al-Rashid (*Kashf al-Mahjub*).

on one's shortcomings despite all the blessings of Allah—this generates a feeling of shame."

A wise man said, "There are five fortresses one has to cross before attaining *taqwa* (obedience or fear of Allah). (1) Accepting hardship instead of blessings, (2) accepting labor instead of comfort, (3) accepting obedience to self-pride, (4) accepting silence to useless talks and (5) accepting death to life."

(1) Secret discussion shields mysteries. (2) Charity protects wealth. (3) Sincerity safeguards deeds. (4) Truth safeguards speech. (5) Consultation safeguards inferences.
— Muhammad (s)

One has to face five things in his pursuit of wealth: (1) physical labor to earn and preserve wealth, (2) abstinence from remembrance of Allah due to his anxiety over wealth, (3) restlessness over his wealth getting stolen, (4) the epithet of a miser, and (5) detachment from the company of righteous people. — Muhammad (s)

One is blessed with five things when he is not concerned with wealth: (1) physical comfort, (2) devotion to the remembrance of Allah having been freed from anxiety over wealth, (3) relief from the fear of theft, (4) good reputation, and (5) company of the righteous people. — Muhammad (s)

In this age whoever has wealth will have five qualities: (1) high aspirations, (2) excessive greed, (3) extreme miserliness, (4) lack of piety (*wara'*), and (5) forgetfulness of the Hereafter. — Sufyan al-Thawri

An Arab poet wrote:
"O men of the world! Know that kinship with this world is temporary
For she is always seeking new companions.
Relation with this world is like that with an unfaithful wife
Who leaves her husband and finds a new one.
Have you still kept your relationship with this world
While she is the worst assassin of those who seek her?
O the seekers of this world, collect provision for your death,
For she is always calling out that (one day) you have to leave this world."

❁❁❁❁

Hastiness is from Satan except in five matters which are *Sunnah* of Rasulullah (s). These are: (1) feeding the guest as soon as possible, (2) burying the dead as soon as possible, (3) arranging the marriage of a daughter as soon as she is of marital age, (4) paying off the debt as soon as possible, and

(5) repenting for the sins committed as soon as possible. — Hatim al-Assam

⁂

Satan was condemned for five reasons. (1) He did not confess his sin. (2) He did not repent for his sin. (3) He did not condemn his carnal self. (4) He did not beg forgiveness for his sin. (5) He despaired of the Mercy from Allah. — Muhammad bin Dawri

⁂

Adam (*a.s.*) was favored for five reasons. (1) He confessed to his sin. (2) He repented for his sin. (3) He condemned his carnal self. (4) He begged forgiveness for his sin. (5) He did not despair of the Mercy from Allah. — Muhammad bin Dawri

⁂

O mankind, do your deeds by regarding the five characteristics as important: (1) serve Allah as much as your needs are for His grace, (2) acquire

AL-MUNABBIHAT

as much belongings as you would require for your life in this world, (3) commit as much sins as you can endure His punishments, (4) take as much provisions for the grave as you would require, and (5) do as much good and virtuous deeds as you would require to live in the Paradise. — Shaqiq Balkhi (r)[34]

᠅

(1) I looked at all my friends, but did not find one better than controlling my tongue. (2) I thought about all kinds of dresses, but did not find one better than the dress of piety. (3) I thought about all kinds of wealth, but did not find anything better in wealth than being contented with little. (4) I thought about all kinds of virtuous deeds, but did not find anything better than giving good advice. (5) I looked at all kinds of delicious foods, but did not find one better than *sabr* (patience). — 'Umar

---

34. Abu 'Ali Shaqiq bin Ibrahim al-Azdi al-Balkhi, a man of wide learning, began his career as a merchant but later turned to the ascetic way. He lived during the reign of the 'Abbasid ruler, Harun al-Rashid, and wrote many books. He learned the Sufi way from Ibrahim bin Adham and taught Hatim Assam. He made the pilgrimage to Makkah and participated in *jihad* in which he was martyred in 194 AH.

The Counsel

An *'abid* (devotee) used to make the following supplications to Allah: "(1) O my God, I have been cheated by high aspirations. (2) Worldly love has ruined me. (3) Satan has led me astray. (4) *Nafs al-ammarah* (the soul that is prone to evil) has obstructed me from doing the right things, and (5) my bad companions have encouraged me to commit sin. O the Lord who hears grievances! Listen to my grievances and be kind to me. If You do not bestow Your mercy on me, then who is there but You to bestow mercy on me?"

O my God! My nights do not end up in happiness without my *munajah* (supplications) to You. My days do not end up in happiness without servitude to You. This world cannot please me without *zikr* (remembrance) of You. There is no happiness in *Akhirah* (the Next World) without a boon from You. And there is no peace or happiness in Paradise without meeting You. — Yahya bin Muʻadh al-Razi

6

There are six things that are barren, ineffectual or helpless (lit. *gharib*) in six places. (1) That mosque is barren in which prayer is not established by its own community. (2) That house is barren in which the Qur'an is not recited. (3) The Qur'an with a transgressor (lit. *fasiq*) is ineffectual (for he does not follow its instructions). (4) That pious Muslim lady is helpless who is controlled by an unfaithful and oppressive husband. (5) That pious Muslim man is helpless who is controlled by an unchaste wife. (6) That religious scholar is helpless whose counsel is disregarded by his own community. Allah will not be merciful with these groups of people on the Day of Judgment. — Muhammad (*s*)

જાજાજા

I have cursed six types of people, and so did Allah and the prophets before me. They are: (1) those who corrupted Allah's Scriptures by either addition or omission; (2) those who do not believe in Allah's decree or predestination (lit. *taqdir*); (3) those usurpers of power who honor those who are cursed by Allah and disrespect those who are honored by Allah; (4) those who consume *haram* (unlawful things) thinking that those are *halal* (lawful) for them; (5) those who consider oppressing my community (lit. *ummah*) as lawful while the same has been made unlawful for them; and (6) those who will leave my customs (lit. *sunnah*). These (six) types of people will not be looked upon favorably on the Day of Judgment by Allah. — Muhammad (s)

≈≈≈≈

Abu Bakr used to caution his soul by saying, "Surely Iblis (Satan) is standing in front of you. Your *nafs* or carnal soul is on your right and *hawa'* or passion is on your left while this material world (lit. *dunya*) is behind you. The organs of your body surround you and the Almighty, through His power and not by occupation of place, is above you. The accursed Satan is inviting you to leave your religion. *Nafs* is inviting you to disobedience (lit.

ma'siyah). *Hawa'* is arousing all sorts of desires in you. *Dunya* is inviting you to prefer her instead of *Akhirah* (Next World). The body organs are inviting you to commit sin. And the Almighty is inviting you to Paradise and forgiveness just as the Qur'an says: "And Allah calls you to Paradise (lit. *Jannah*) and forgiveness (lit. *maghfirah*)." Therefore, whoever accepts the invitation of Satan, his religion will be ruined. Whoever accepts the invitation of *nafs* or carnal soul, his *ruh* or spirit will be ruined. Whoever accepts the invitation of *hawa'* will have his morality lost. Whoever accepts the invitation of the *dunya* will lose *Akhirah* (Next World). Whoever accepts the invitation of his organs will lose Paradise. And whoever accepts the invitation of Allah, all his sins will be erased and he will gain all goodness."

Allah has kept six things in six others: (1) His pleasure in servitude or obedience; (2) His anger in (committing) sin; (3) *Ism al-'Azim* (the most Glorious name of Allah) within the Qur'an; (4) *Shab al-Qadr* (the Night of Power) in (the month of) Ramadan; (5) *Salah al-Wusta* (middle prayer) among *salah* (prescribed prayers); and (6) *Qiyamah* (the Doomsday) among (His) days. — 'Umar

Surely the true believers go through six types of anxieties: (1) fear of Allah, the Exalted, that they might lose their faith (for having done something which may not have been right), (2) fear of the two recording angels that they have recorded something which will put them into disgrace on the Day of Judgment, (3) anxiety about Satan that he might waste all their good deeds (by enticing them into committing sin), (4) fear of the angel of death that he could come anytime to snatch their lives while they are still unprepared, (5) anxiety about this world that they might be deceived by it and therefore lose the benefits of the Next World, and (6) anxiety about family members that their company might distract them from remembrance of Allah. — 'Uthman

Whoever acquires six qualities will enter Paradise and will be saved from the Hell Fire. These are: (1) whoever has attained *ma'rifah* (mystical knowledge) of Allah serves Him. (2) Whoever has the knowledge of Satan defies him. (3) Whoever has the knowledge of *Akhirah* (the Next World) desires it. (4) Whoever has the knowledge of *dunya* (this world) rejects it. (5) Whoever knows the truth follows it. (6) Whoever knows the falsehood shuns it. — 'Ali

There are six blessings: (1) Islam, (2) Qur'an, (3) Muhammad (*s*), the Messenger of Allah, (4) security, (5) concealment of shortcomings, and (6) self-sufficiency. — 'Ali

There are six things that support six other things: (1) knowledge guides deeds; (2) intelligence aids knowledge; (3) wisdom leads to good deeds; (4) passion leads to sin; (5) wealth is a garment of the

proud; (6) this world is a market place for (searching) the Hereafter.
— Yahya bin Mu'adh al-Razi

Six things are equally priceless anywhere in this world. These are: (1) the food which is easily digestible, (2) righteous children, (3) a likable wife, (4) eloquent and plain (lit. *muhkam*) speech, (5) wisdom, and (6) a healthy body. — Abu Dharr Jamhar

(1) Were it not for the devotees (lit. *'abdal*), the world would have collapsed with all its contents. (2) Were it not for the righteous people (lit. *salihun*), all the evildoers would have perished. (3) Were it not for the learned men of religion (lit. *'ulama'*), everyone would have turned into beasts. (4) Were it not for the rulers there would be no ceasing of bloodshed. (5) Were it not for laymen, this world would have remained uncultivable. (6) Were it not for the wind everything would have

rotted! — Hassan al-Basri

❦❦❦

A wise man said, "(1) He who does not fear Allah will not be saved from uttering foul words. (2) He who does not have any fear about the Day of Judgment will not be able to avoid forbidden and doubtful things. (3) He who aspires for wealth will not be able to save himself from greed. (4) He who cannot safeguard his deeds will not be able to save himself from pride (lit. *riya'*). (5) He who does not seek Allah's help for safeguarding his heart (lit. *qalb*) will not be able to save himself from envy (lit. *hasad*). (6) He who considers himself to be more knowledgeable and virtuous will not be able to save himself from self-conceit."

❦❦❦

Surely, the heart (lit. *qalb*) is polluted by six things. These are: (1) indulgence in transgression in the hope of repenting later (for forgiveness); (2) actions that do not follow acquired knowledge; (3) deeds that are done without sincerity; (4)

ingratitude to Allah despite His provisions (*rizq*); (5) discontentment with the Decree of Allah; and (6) heedlessness (in taking necessary lessons) even after burying the dead. — Hassan al-Basri

❧❧❧

Whoever prefers this world to the Next will be humiliated by Allah in six ways: three in this world and three in the Next World. Those of this world are: (1) lack of contentment, (2) extreme greed or avarice, and (3) displeasure in worship. Those of the Next World are: (1) extreme fear on the Day of Judgment, (2) hard accounting (on the Day of Judgment), and (3) lasting remorse.
— Hassan al-Basri

❧❧❧

(1) There is no peace of mind for an envier. (2) There is no sympathy for a liar. (3) There is no salvation for a miser. (4) There is no guarantee for fulfillment of kingly vows. (5) There is no stability for a corrupt regime. (6) There is no change in the destiny (lit. *taqdir*) fixed by Allah.

AL-MUNABBIHAT

— Ahnaf bin Qays (r)[35]

Once a wise man was asked about how one could discern if his repentance was accepted or rejected. He replied, "I am not qualified enough to comment on that. However, there are some signs of one's repentance being accepted. These are: (1) the person whose repentance is accepted always assumes that he is still vulnerable to committing sin. (2) His heart is not at peace but is worried about finding salvation in the Next World. (3) He looks out for the company of pious men and seclusion from impious people. (4) He considers

---

35. Ahnaf bin Qays, a Basran noble of the tribe of Tamim, was instrumental in his tribe's conversion to Islam. He was a *tabi'i*, a successor, who met the Prophet's companion Abu Dharr al-Ghifari. He was the chief of the Banu Tamim. Al-Ahnaf was known for being a prudent and eloquent leader. A notable General, he participated in the conquest of Persia. He invaded Khurasan under the leadership of Abu Musa al-Ash'ari., and later served as its governor. He withdrew from the dissension that broke out following the Battle of the Camel, but supported 'Ali bin Abi Talib in the Battle of Siffin, and disagreed with 'Ali over his choosing Abu Musa al-Ash'ari as his representative in the Arbitration. Al-Ahnaf insisted on his opposition to Mu'awiyah even after Mu'awiyah assumed the caliphate. Politically influential, he was noted for his wisdom, and his forbearance became proverbial among the Arabs. Many maxims and aphorisms are attributed to him. He died around 687 AD (67 AH).

The Counsel

little wealth of this world to be colossal and his great many virtuous deeds for the Hereafter as meager. (5) He concentrates on obeying Allah's command and remains indifferent about matters whose responsibility lies with Allah. (6) He controls his tongue, is ever repentant and worried about (his status in) the Next World."

In my opinion, major stupidity lies in (1) continuing sinful acts without genuine repentance in the hope that these will be forgiven, (2) desiring Allah's intimacy without servitude, (3) hoping to eat foods of Paradise while sowing the seeds of Hell (lit. *Nar* or Fire), (4) desiring to enter Paradise while engaged in His disobedience, (5) expecting rewards without doing good deeds, and (6) expecting Allah's mercy while transgressing the limits imposed by Him. — Yahya bin Mu'adh al-Razi

Ahnaf bin Qays was asked (six questions): (1) "Of

all the blessings of Allah, what is the best for the slave (of Allah)?" He replied, "Inherent wisdom." (2) "What next, if it is not there?" — "Noble manners." (3) "What if it is not there?" — "Agreeable friend." (4) "What if it is not there?" — "Meditating heart." (5) "What if that is not there?" — "Prolonged silence." (6) "What if that is not there?" — "Contemplation that death is near."

7

On the Day of Judgment, when there will not be any other shade available, Allah, the Exalted, will provide shade to seven types of people under His Throne. These are: (1) a just ruler, (2) a young man who spent his youth in worship of Allah, the Exalted, (3) a person who is dedicated to the remembrance of Allah in seclusion and sheds tears in fear of Him, (4) a person who is attached to mosque such that he anxiously awaits the calling of the next *adhan* (call of prayer) (so that he again returns for prayer there), (5) a person who secretly spends money in charity, (6) those two persons who love each other for the sake of Allah, and (7) a person who refuses the temptation from a beautiful damsel to commit fornication by saying, "I truly fear Allah, the Exalted." — Muhammad (s), narrated by Abu Hurayrah

AL-MUNABBIHAT

A miser shall surely fall into any of the seven calamities: (1) after his death, his wealth (lit. *mal*) may be owned by his inheritors, and they spend it through disobedience of Allah; (2) his wealth may be confiscated by an oppressive ruler; (3) he may waste all his savings in fulfilling the demands of his carnal self; (4) he may decide to spend all his money on building a house in an uncultivable land; (5) several types of worldly disasters may anytime strike him or his wealth, e.g., drowning, fire, robbery, etc.; (6) he may be struck by a disease that will consume all his wealth to find the cure; (7) he may hide his money in a place about which he later does not have any recollection of.
— Abu Bakr as-Siddiq

(1) Whoever is given to much merry-making (or makes too much jokes) will lose people's respect. (2) He who belittles others will find himself belittled. (3) Whoever is very adept in something will earn fame because of that. (4) Whoever talks too much, often talks nonsense. (5) Whoever talks nonsense will have his shyness and modesty

The Counsel

diminished. (6) Whoever is immodest will have his piety diminished. (7) He whose piety is diminished will have his heart dying. — 'Umar

۞۞۞

These seven lines were engraved on the golden plate called *al-Kanz*: "(1) How strange is the man who knows death, yet spends his time happy and gay. (2) How strange is the man who knows that the world is temporary, yet falls into her love. (3) How strange is the man who knows that everything that happens in this world is as per Allah's decree (lit. *taqdir*), yet is saddened by losses. (4) How strange is the man who knows that he will be called to account on the Day of Judgment, yet goes after amassing wealth. (5) How strange is the man who knows the (severity of punishment in) Hell, yet goes on committing sin. (6) How strange is the man who knows Allah well, yet seeks help from objects other than Him! (7) How strange is the man who knows well about Paradise, yet seeks pleasure in this world, and knows that Satan is his eternal enemy and yet follows him!" — 'Uthman

'Ali was asked, "(1) What is heavier than the sky? (2) What is wider than the earth? (3) What is deeper than the ocean? (4) What is harder than stone? (5) What is hotter than fire? (6) What is colder than ice? (7) What is bitterer than poison?" In reply, he said, "(1) To vilify someone is heavier than the sky. (2) Truth is wider than the earth. (3) The heart of a contented person is deeper than the ocean. (4) The heart of a hypocrite (lit. *munafiq*) is harder than a stone. (5) An oppressive ruler is hotter than fire. (6) A miser's heart is colder than ice (lit. help from a miser is colder than ice). (7) Being steadfast during hardships is more bitter than poison (elsewhere, backbiting is more bitter than poison)."

(1) Jibril (*a.s.*) has advised me so much about the rights of neighbors that I was beginning to wonder if I were to include them as my inheritors. (2) He advised me so often about the rights of wives that I was beginning to think that divorce would be

forbidden. (3) He has advised me so much about ensuring the rights of slaves that I was wondering if slavery was going to be abolished soon and if they would be all freed. (4) He has exhorted me so much about the use of *miswak* (tooth stick to clean teeth) that I was wondering if its use would become obligatory. (5) He has exhorted me to pray in congregation so much so that I was beginning to think that Allah would not accept prayers that are performed without congregation. (6) He has exhorted me so much about passing nights in prayers that I was wondering if sleep during night would be forbidden. (7) He has exhorted me so much on doing *zikr* (remembrance) of Allah that I was beginning to think that all kinds of talks except *zikr* were useless. — Muhammad (s), narrated by Jabir bin 'Abdullah

❧❧❧❧

On the Day of Judgment, Allah will not glance with mercy over seven categories of people and they will be thrown into Hell. These are: (1) those who engage in adultery, (2) those who masturbate, (3) those who engage in sex with beasts, (4) those who engage in anal sex with their wives, (5) those who marry the daughters of their wives (with whom they had sex), (6) those who commit adultery with their neighbors' wives, and (7) those who trouble their neighbors. — Muhammad (s)

There are seven categories of people who will be considered as martyrs without being martyred in the path of Allah. These are: (1) those who died of diarrhea, (2) those who died of drowning, (3) those who died of paralysis, (4) those who died of small pox, (5) those who were killed due to fire, (6) those who died of being pressed under weight (like in an earthquake), and (7) those who died while giving birth to their children. — Muhammad (s)

It is incumbent upon wise men to prefer seven things by discarding seven other things: (1) preferring poverty over wealth, (2) preferring humility over honor and prestige, (3) preferring modesty over pride and glory, (4) preferring

The Counsel

hunger over gluttony, (5) preferring contemplation over merry-making, (6) preferring lowliness over greatness or vanity, and (7) preferring death to life.
— 'Abdullah bin 'Abbas

8

There are eight things that are not gratified with eight other things. These are: (1) eye is not gratified by sight, (2) earth is not satiated with rain, (3) woman with man, (4) the scholar with knowledge, (5) the beggars with alms, (6) avaricious with the amassing of wealth, (7) the ocean with water, and (8) fire with wood.
— Muhammad (s)

※※※

There are eight things that beautify eight other things: (1) Purity and piety beautify poverty. (2) Gratitude beautifies blessings. (3) Patience (lit. *sabr*) beautifies adversity. (4) Forbearance (lit. *hilm*) beautifies knowledge (lit. *'ilm*). (5) Sobriety and obedience beautify student. (6) Much weeping beautifies fear (of Allah). (7) Grace without any expectation beautifies generosity (lit. *ihsan*). (8) Humbleness (lit. *khushu'*) beautifies prayer.

The Counsel

— Abu Bakr as-Siddiq

❧❧❧❧

(1) Whoever shuns vain talks gains wisdom. (2) Whoever has control over the roving eyes attains humility and humbleness (lit. *khushu'*) of the heart (lit. *qalb*). (3) Whoever shuns gluttony attains the true taste of *'ibadah* (worship). (4) Whoever shuns revelry gains respect. (5) Whoever shuns jokes his face is illuminated. (6) Whoever shuns this world gains love of the Hereafter. (7) Whoever refrains from finding faults with others gains the power of self-rectification. (8) Whoever refrains from finding flaws with the mysteries and signs of Allah the Exalted attains salvation from hypocrisy.
— 'Umar

❧❧❧❧

There are eight signs of the men of gnosis. Their hearts are (simultaneously) filled with hope and fear. Their tongues are saturated with praise and adoration of Allah. Their eyes are filled with abashment and tears. Their desire is to shun worldly cravings and earn the pleasure of their Master (Allah). — 'Uthman

❧❧❧

(1) That prayer which lacks *khushu'* (humility and humbleness) has no merit. (2) That fasting which does not refrain one from forbidden things has no merit. (3) That recital (of the Qur'an) which does not arouse contemplation has no merit. (4) That knowledge which lacks piety (*wara'*) has no merit. (5) That wealth out of which no charity is made is worthless. (6) That brotherhood which does not safeguard the honor of others has no merit. (7) That blessing which does not last has no merit. (8) That supplication (lit. *du'a*) which lacks sincerity has no merit. — 'Ali

9

Allah, the Exalted, revealed to Musa (*a.s.*) through the Tawrah (Torah) that the roots of all evils are three: (1) pride, (2) envy, and (3) greed. From these three six other vices originate: (1) gluttony, (2) excessive sleep, (3) comfort (*rahah*), (4) love of wealth, (5) love for admiration and praise, and (6) love for leadership or power. — Muhammad (*s*)

※※※

There are three kinds of worshippers. And each of these worshippers has three types of signs. For example, (1) one group worships Allah out of fear of Him, (2) another group worships Him in order that their wishes may come true, and (3) the third group worships Him because of their love. The signs of the first group are: (1) they know the evil nature of their soul (lit. *nafs*), (2) they consider their good deeds to be too few, and (3) they assume their sins to be too many. The signs of the second group are: (1) they are guides of mankind, (2) of all people in this world they are the most generous in their spending of wealth in the path of Allah, and (3) of all people they are the most optimistic people in their relation to Allah. The signs of the third group are: (1) they donate all their good portions in order to please Allah, (2) they are constantly at war against their *nafs* (soul) in order to earn His pleasure, and (3) they are always engaged in carrying out commands and prohibitions of Allah. — Abu Bakr as-Siddiq

Surely, Satan has nine kinds of descendants. These are: (1) *zalitun*, (2) *wasinun*, (3) *laqusun*, (4) *a'wanun*, (5) *haffafun*, (6) *murratun*, (7) *musawwitun*, (8) *dasimun*, and (9) *wal-hanun*. (Everyone is assigned to his or her own task.) (1) *Zalitun* are assigned to market places with the task of enticing people into altercations and quarrels there. (2) *Wasinun* are assigned with the task of putting people into calamities. (3) *Laqusun* are assigned to encourage people to worship false gods (like idols). (4) *A'wanun* encourage rulers to do

The Counsel

evil deeds. (5) *Haffafun* encourage people to get intoxicated (with drugs and alcohol). (6) *Murratun* draw people to lottery or games of chances, dance and music, etc. (7) *Musawwitun* are assigned to propagating rumors. (8) *Dasimun* are assigned to create division among the family members who enter their homes without seeking protection from Allah. (9) *Wal-hanun* are responsible for creating doubts among worshippers. — 'Umar

❧❧❧

Those who regularly pray the five daily prayers on time, Allah bestows nine favors on them. These are: (1) Allah loves them; (2) they enjoy good health; (3) the Angels protect them; (4) their homes are blessed; (5) their faces show signs of piety; (6) Allah softens their *qalb* (i.e., they become tender-hearted); (7) they will cross the bridge of *Sirat* with lightning speeds; (8) they will be saved from the Hell Fire; and (9) their neighbors in Paradise will be those people about whom Allah has said, "On them shall be no fear, nor shall they grieve" (Qur'an 2:38) — 'Uthman

Tears are shed for three reasons: (1) fear of Allah's punishment, (2) fear of earning His displeasure, and (3) fear of separation from Him. The first kind (of tears) compensates for one's sins, the second obliterates one's faults, and the third earns Allah's proximity with pleasure. As a result of sins being forgiven the person is saved from punishment. As a result of faults being obliterated the person attains permanent bliss and high status in the Next World. As a result of earning Allah's pleasure and intimacy the person is blessed with the vision of Allah, granted the visitation of the angels and is given the tiding of high honor. — 'Ali

10

The Prophet (*s*) said, "You should use tooth stick (*miswak*) (to brush your teeth) because there are ten benefits in its use. (1) It cleans your mouth. (2) You earn the pleasure of Allah. (3) Satan gets disappointed in you. (4) Allah and His Angels love you. (5) It strengthens the gum of your teeth. (6) It clears cough. (7) Your mouth smells good. (8) It is good for your gall bladder. (9) It enhances your eyesight. (10) It removes bad odors from your mouth and it is my way (lit. Sunnah) (to use *miswak*)." He then continued by saying, "It is seventy times more rewarding to pray after brushing the teeth than to pray without."

Whoever is blessed with ten qualities by Allah will be saved from all kinds of trials and tribulations and will be included among the *muqarrabin* (those who are brought near Him) and *mutaqqin* (God-

fearing ones). These qualities are: (1) uncompromising truthfulness combined with undaunted trust in Allah's decree; (2) fortitude (lit. *sabr*) combined with gratitude (lit. *shukr*); (3) acceptance of poverty with the rejection of worldly life in order to worship Him; (4) contemplation (lit. *fikr*) with an empty stomach; (5) constant anxiety (about the Hereafter) combined with fear of Allah; (6) continuous supplication to Allah through tears and humility; (7) clemency combined with kindness of heart; (8) bashfulness while consumed in Allah's love; (9) immense patience combined with useful knowledge; and (10) unfailing faith with deep erudition.
— Abu Bakr as-Siddiq

ෂ෴෴

Ten things do not become worthy without ten other things. For example, (1) wisdom (lit. *'aql*) without piety (lit. *wara'*); (2) bounty, grace or dignity (lit. *fadl*) without knowledge (lit. *'ilm*); (3) success without fear (of Allah); (4) authority (lit. *sultanah*) without justice (lit. *'adl*); (5) aristocracy without manners (lit. *adab*); (6) happiness without

The Counsel

peace or security; (7) wealth without liberality (lit. *jud*); (8) asceticism or sainthood without self-denial or contentment with little (lit. *qana'ah*); (9) high status without politeness or sobriety; and (10) *jihad* without arms. — 'Umar

There are ten completely useless things: (1) that learned person to whom no question is asked; (2) that knowledge which is not put to use; (3) that thoughtful decision which is not acted upon; (4) that weapon which is not used; (5) that mosque where prayers are not established; (6) that Qur'an which is not recited; (7) that wealth which is not spent in the right path; (8) that horse which is not ridden; (9) that knowledge of piety gained (solely) for seeking the *dunya* (material world); (10) that long life which failed to earn the necessary provisions for the Next World. — 'Uthman

(1) Knowledge is the best bequest (lit. *mirath*); (2) manner (lit. *adab*) is the best transaction; (3) fear

of Allah (lit. *taqwa*) is the best possession; (4) worship (lit. *'ibadah*) is the best capital; (5) virtuous deeds are the best guides; (6) noble character is the best companion; (7) patience is the best minister; (8) self-denial or contentment in little (lit. *qana'ah*) is the best treasure; (9) success (lit. *tawfiq*) is the best aid; and (10) death is the best teacher of manners. — 'Ali

❧❧❧

Ten groups of people from within my community (*ummah*) will become infidels to Allah the Great, though they will assume that they were true believers. These are: (1) murderers, (2) sorcerers (3) those who are unabashed of their wives' associations with other men, (4) those who deny the poor-due (lit. *zakat*), (5) drunkards, (6) those who deliberately neglect performing the hajj (pilgrimage), (7) mischief-makers or those who persecute (others), (8) the arms-dealers to the enemies of Muslims, (9) men who engage in anal sex with their wives, and (10) those who marry women that are forbidden unto them.
— Muhammad (s)

The Counsel

Not a single slave in the heavens and the earth will be accepted as a true believer as long as: (1) he/she has not gained Allah's intimacy; (2) he/she cannot gain Allah's intimacy until he/she is a Muslim; (3) he/she is not a Muslim as long as other people are not safe from the harms of his/her hands and mouths; (4) (again) he/she is not a Muslim as long as he/she has no knowledge (in essential matters); (5) he/she will not be considered knowledgeable as long as he/she does not practice what he/she learned; (6) he/she will not be able to practice what he/she learned until he/she becomes an ascetic (lit. *zahid*); (7) he/she will not be included among the ascetics as long as he/she does not practice piety or abstinence (lit. *wara'*); (8) he/she will not be able to practice piety as long as he/she is not humble and gentle; (9) he/she will not become humble as long as he/she has no knowledge of (the evil of) his/her own soul (lit. *nafs*); and (10) he/she will not be able to know his/her own soul as long as he/she is not well-versed in theology (lit. *kalam*). — Muhammad (s)

AL-MUNABBIHAT

Yahya bin Mu'adh al-Razi once told a worldly jurist, "O the (so-called) scholar of religion and Sunnah, (1) your palaces are like those of the Roman emperors (Caesar), (2) your houses are like those of the Persian emperors (Cyrus), (3) your dwelling places are like those of Korah (Qarun), (4) your gates are like those of Saul (Talut), (5) your dresses are like those of Goliath (Jalut), (6) your doctrine is that of Satan, (7) your furniture is like those of Mardiyah, (8) your regime is like that of the Pharaoh, (9) your leaders are materialistic, bribe-takers and dishonest people, and (10) your death is that of ignorance. Where is the custom of Muhammad in you?"

A wise man said, "Allah, the Exalted, dislikes ten habits in ten types of people: (1) stinginess among the rich; (2) pride among the poor; (3) covetousness (lit. *tama'*) among the religious scholars (lit. *'ulama'*); (4) shamelessness among the women; (5) worldly love among the old; (6)

The Counsel

laziness among the young; (7) oppression from the rulers; (8) cowardliness among the warriors; (9) vanity or self-conceit (lit. *'ujb*) (of one's asceticism) among the ascetics (lit. *zahid*); (10) pride (lit. *riya'*) among the devotees (lit. *'ubbad*)."

❧❧❧

Security is of ten types: five of these are in this world and the other five in the Next World. Those of this world are: (1) knowledge (lit. *'ilm*), (2) worship (lit. *'ibadah*), (3) (earning) a lawful livelihood, (4) endurance and steadfastness (lit. *sabr*) during trials and tribulations, and (5) gratitude (lit. *shukr*) (to Allah) for (His) blessings. Those of the Next World are: (1) finding the Angel of Death in his compassionate and polite mood when he arrives to take away life, (2) not being frightened by the Angels Munkar and Nakir (during questioning) in the grave, (3) being safe and secure on the horrifying Day of Judgment, (4) receiving forgiveness of sins and acceptance of good deeds, and (5) crossing the Bridge (*Sirat*) at the speed of lightning and entrance into paradise peacefully. — Muhammad (*s*)

AL-MUNABBIHAT

Allah the Exalted has given ten names to His Scripture: (1) the Qur'an, (2) Furqan, (3) Kitab, (4) Tanzil, (5) Huda, (6) Nur, (7) Rahmah, (8) Ruh, (9) Shafa'ah and (10) Zikr. The names Qur'an, Furqan, Kitab and Tanzil are well-known. As far as the names Huda, Nur, Rahmah and Shafa'ah are concerned, Allah the Exalted says, "O mankind, an admonition from your Lord has come, and there is a healing (lit. *shafa'ah*) for your chest and a guidance (lit. *huda*) and a mercy (lit. *rahmah*) for the true believers. And a light (lit. *nur*) and Book (lit. *kitab*) that makes things clear has come down to you from Allah." Regarding Ruh, Allah says, "And similarly I have revealed to you that the Spirit (lit. *ruh*) is by My command." As to the name Zikr, Allah says, "And I have revealed the Remembrance (lit. *zikr*) to you in order that you may explain this to mankind." — Abu al-Fadl (r)[36]

---

36. Probably referring to Abu al-Fadl Hassan Sarakhsi, who was the teacher of Shaykh Abu Sa'id Abu al-Khayr. He is mentioned as a saint in Farid al-Din's *Tadhkirah al-Awiya'* (Memoirs of the Saints).

The Counsel

Luqman Hakim told his son, "My son, genuine wisdom (lit. *hikmah*) lies in ten deeds. These are: (1) reviving a dead heart; (2) associating (lit. sit or live) with the needy (lit. *miskin*); (3) avoiding the company of rulers; (4) honoring the downtrodden (lit. *wadiya*); (5) emancipating the slaves; (6) sheltering the wayfarers or strangers (lit. *gharib*); (7) enriching the poor; (8) honoring the respectable people (*sharif*); (9) giving leadership to (deserving) leaders. (10) ...[37] "

☙☙☙

A wise man said, "Whenever an intelligent person vows to make repentance, he should inculcate ten qualities right away. These are: (1) beseeching Allah's forgiveness verbally; (2) being truly ashamed at heart (of his deeds); (3) protecting the body from (further) committing sins; (4) firmly resolving never to re-engage in committing sins; (5) loving the Hereafter; (6) feeling enmity towards this world; (7) controlling the tongue; (8-9) eating

---

37. The tenth advice is not mentioned in the text.

and drinking less in favor of learning and worship; and (10) sleeping less for Allah praises His slaves in the Qur'an by saying: 'They used to sleep little at night and seek Allah's forgiveness in the later hours of the night.' "

༄༅༄༅

Everyday the earth admonishes human beings ten times by saying: "O Children of Adam: (1) You roam over my back, do you know that one day you will come inside my belly? (2) You commit all kinds of sins over my back, but you will be punished inside my belly. (3) You laugh over my back, but will cry inside me. (4) You are enjoying life over my back, but will be in despair inside my belly. (5) You accumulate wealth over my back, but will repent inside me. (6) You consume *haram* (forbidden things) over my back, but will be consumed by insects, snakes and scorpions inside my belly. (7) You take pride in yourself over my back, but will be humiliated inside me. (8) You are enjoying comfort over my back, but will suffer terribly inside me. (9) You walk in the daylight (and skylight) over my back, but will reside in the

The Counsel

darkness of my belly. (10) You march in groups over my back, but will reside alone inside me."
— Anas bin Malik (r)[38]

❧❧❧

The man who spends his time in amusement (neglecting his duties) will be afflicted with ten types of punishments. These are: (1) his *qalb* (heart) will die; (2) the radiance of his appearance will diminish; (3) Satan will be pleased with him; (4) Allah, the Most Merciful, will be angry with him; (5) he will be troubled on the Day of Judgment with severe accounting; (6) the Prophet (s) will turn his face away from him on the Day of Judgment; (7) the angels will curse him; (8) he will be despised by all the inhabitants of the heavens and the earth; (9) he will forget everything; and (10) he will be humiliated on the Day of Judgment.
— Muhammad (s)

---

38. Anas bin Malik was a personal caretaker of the Prophet (s) from the time he migrated to Madinah till his death. He narrated many Prophetic traditions. During 'Uthman's caliphate he moved to Basrah and settled there establishing the Basran school of Islamic learning. He died at an advanced age of 103 in 93 AH in Basrah. When he died there was not a single surviving companion of the Prophet except Abu Tufayl.

AL-MUNABBIHAT

Hassan al-Basri said, "One day while I was roaming the streets and the shopping centers in Basrah with a young devotee (lit. *'abid*), we came across a doctor. He was sitting on a chair and there were many men and women, young and old, who were sitting in front of him. Each one of them was holding a jar of water. They came there to find medicine for their sickness. The young devotee approached the doctor and asked him, 'O doctor, do you have any medicine that removes sin and cures the sickness of the heart (lit. *qalb*)?' When the doctor replied in the affirmative the devotee said, 'Then give it to me.' The doctor replied, 'Take ten things from me (to cure your sickness). (These are:) (1) Take a root of the tree of poverty (lit. *faqr*) and some roots of the tree of humility. (2) Mix these with the turmeric of repentance (lit. *tawbah*) in the (3) grindstone of Allah's pleasure (lit. *rida*). And then (4) grind the mixture with the iron grinder of contentment (lit. *qana'ah*) in Allah's decree (lit. *qadr*). (5) Then put the mixture in a bowl of piety. (6) Pour the water of humiliation (lit. *haya*) over the mixture and (7) boil it with the

The Counsel

fire of love (lit. *mahabbah*). (8) Then pour the (hot) solution into the cup of gratitude (lit. *shukr*) and (9) cool it off with the fan of hope of Allah's mercy. (10) (Finally) drink the medicine with the spoon of praise (lit. *hamd*) of Allah. Truly, if you follow this prescription, all your sickness will be cured and you will benefit from all the troubles both in this world and the Hereafter.'"

☙❦❧

Once upon a time a king summoned five scholars and wise men and requested them to say words of wisdom. Each one of them spoke two sentences thus totaling ten sentences. The first one to speak said, "Security lies in fear of Allah and infidelity in not fearing Him. Freedom lies in not fearing the creation (lit. *makhluq*) and bondage in fearing such." The second one spoke, "To place hope in Allah is such richness that no scarcity can harm it. And to despair of Allah is such poverty that no wealth can benefit it." The third one spoke, "The richness of the heart cannot be harmed by any poverty. And the poverty of the heart cannot be enriched by anything." The fourth wise man said,

"The richness of the heart is further enriched by making charity. And the poverty of the heart is impoverished despite all the riches." The fifth man spoke, "It is better to have some decency than to forsake all evil. And it is better to forsake all evil than to have some decency."

❧❧❧

Ibn 'Abbas related that the Prophet (s) said, "Ten categories of people from my community will not enter Paradise without making repentance. They are: (1) the *qalla'*, (2) *jayyuf*, (3) *qattat*, (4) *dabbub*, (5) *dayyuth*, (6) *sahib al-'artahah*, (7) *sahib al-kubah*, (8) *'utul*, (9) *zanim* and (10) *'aqq al-walidayn*." (1) He was then asked, "O Messenger of Allah, who is *qalla'*?" He answered, "He spies against laymen on behalf of the rulers." (2) "Who is *jayyuf*?" He answered, "They steal burial shrouds (lit. *kafn*)." (3) "Who is *qattat*?" He answered, "They slander others." (4) "Who is *dabbub*?" He replied, "They gather amoral women in their houses to engage in evil deeds." (5) "Who is *dayyuth*?" He replied, "They do not object to their wives' free-mixing with other men." (6) "Who

The Counsel

is *sahib al-'artahah?*" He answered, "He plays drums." (7) "Who is *sahb al-kubah?*" He replied, "He indulges in musical instruments." (8) "Who is *'utul?*" He replied, "He is that stone-hearted man who neither forgives nor accepts anyone's excuse." (9) "Who is *zanim?*" He replied, "He vilifies others on the street." (10) "Who are *'aqq al-walidayn?*" He replied, "They are disobedient to their parents."

❧❧❧

The prayer of ten categories of people is not accepted by Allah the Exalted. (They are:) (1) The one who prays alone without *qira'ah* (recitation of the Qur'anic verses, e.g., Surah al-Fatihah, as is done by the Imam in a congregational prayer); (2) the one who does not pay *zakah* (poor-due); (3) the Imam who is disliked (by his community); (4) the slave who flees from his master; (5) the person who is addicted to drinking or drugs; (6) the wife who passes the night without pleasing her husband (when he wants cohabitation); (7) the free woman who prays discarding her outer garment (to show her adornments); (8) the person who practices *riba* (usury); (9) the oppressive ruler; and (10) that person whose prayer does not deter him from committing mischief and, thereby, widening the gap between him and Allah. — Muhammad (s)

Those who enter mosques should observe ten manners. (1) Those who enter the mosque with shoes or socks on should make sure that no filth is sticking on these. (2) They should enter with the right foot first. (3) They should make the supplication, "*Allahumm aftah lana abwaba rahmatika innaka anta al-Wahhab* (Meaning: O Allah, open for us the door of Your mercy. You are surely the One who gives reward)." (4) They should salute those who are inside the mosque. But if there is no one inside, they should supplicate, "As-salamu 'alayna wa 'ala 'ibadillahis salhin. Ash-hadu an la ilaha illa Allah, wa anna Muhammad-ur-Rasulullah (Peace be upon me and all the righteous slaves of Allah. I testify that there is no God but Allah and that Muhammad is His Messenger)." (5) They should not move in front of those who are praying. (6) They should not engage in any worldly affair inside the mosque. (7) They should not

The Counsel

engage in vain talks inside the mosque. (8) They should offer two units (lit. *rak'ah*) of prayer (except if the Imam is already leading one of the five daily prayers). (9) They should not enter the mosque without ablution (lit. *wudu'*). (10) They should supplicate (after *wudu'*) while standing, "*Subhanaka Allahumma wa bi hamdika. Ashhadu an la ilaha illa anta astagh-firuka wa atubu ilayka* (Glorified be You, O Allah, and all praises are due to You. I testify that there is no God but You and I seek Your forgiveness and I repent to You)." — Muhammad (s)

❧❧❧

Prayer is the foundation of *din* (religion), and it bestows ten qualities. (These are:) (1) Beauty of appearance, (2) light of the heart, (3) comfort of the body, (4) companionship in the grave, (5) means for the descent of Allah's mercy (*manzil al-rahmah*), (6) key to the heaven, (7) weight of the Scales (Mizan, i.e., the heaviness of balance of good virtues on the Day of Judgment), (8) pleasure of the Lord, (9) investment for Paradise, and (10) curtain for the Hell Fire. Whoever establishes prayer properly has established his religion. And whoever leaves prayer has destroyed (abandoned) his religion. — Muhammad (s), narrated by Abu Hurayrah

When Allah, the Exalted, will desire to let the inhabitants of the Paradise enter Paradise, He will send for them the Angels with heavenly dresses and gifts. When they will intend to enter Paradise, the Angels will ask them to wait and inform them of the gifts from Allah. They will ask, "What kinds of gifts are awaiting us?" The angels will reply, "It is a ring with ten engravings. The first of the engravings will state, 'Peace be upon you; greetings to you for becoming the dwellers of Paradise forever.' The second one will state, 'You have been freed from all kinds of sufferings and anxieties.' The third one will state, 'This is that Garden that you have earned due to your good deeds.' The fourth one will state, 'I have adorned you with heavenly dresses and ornaments.' The fifth one will state, 'I have wed them unto fair ones with wide lovely eyes (lit. *hur*); I have rewarded them for they were steadfast; surely they have succeeded.' The sixth one will state, 'You have earned this reward today for your obedience.' The seventh one will state, 'You have all been given youth and you will never age.' The eighth one will state, 'You have entered the abode of peace and you will never be frightened here.' The ninth one will state, 'You have earned the company of the friends of Allah, the prophets, the truthful ones, the martyrs and the righteous ones (of Allah).' The tenth one will state, 'You are dwelling here as the neighbors of the Merciful (lit. *al-Rahman*), the Owner of the Great Throne.'" After that these people will be allowed to enter Paradise and they will say, "All praise and gratitude is due to Allah, who has removed all our pains and sufferings. Surely He is our Lord, Ever Forgiving and Rewarding to those who work good." They will also say, "All praise is due to Allah who has fulfilled all that He has promised to us. He has made us inhabit this Garden. We may reside wherever we choose. What a great bounty for those who do good deeds!"

And when Allah will desire to let the inhabitants of Hell enter, He will send an angel to them. He will carry a message from Him with ten engraved seals. The first one will state, "Enter the Fire where you will neither die nor live and will never be taken out." The second one will state, "Enter the place of punishment where you will have no comfort." The third one will state, "You have despaired of My Mercy." The fourth one will state, "Suffer pain, sorrow and distress forever." The fifth one will state, "Your garment will be of fire, food—thorny *zaqqum*, drink—hot water, bed and comforter—fire." The sixth one will state, "Because of your disobedience this is your punishment today." The seventh one will state, "My Anger is upon you forever in the Hell." The eighth one will state, "You committed major sins and still you did not repent for your deeds; My curse is upon you." The ninth one will state, "Satan will be your constant companion inside Hell." The tenth one will state, "You followed in the footsteps of Satan and preferred the world to the Hereafter; therefore, this is your punishment." — Muhammad (s), narrated by 'A'ishah

The Counsel

A wise man said, "I sought ten items in ten places but found them in ten other places: (1) I sought honor and dignity in pride, but found them in politeness and gentility. (2) I sought *'ibadah* (worship or servitude) in prayer, but found it in living modestly according to the Law (lit. Shari'ah). (3) I sought comfort in luxurious living, but found it in *zuhud* (discarding worldly comfort). (4) I sought the light of my heart in daytime prayers, but found it in (secret) late night prayers. (5) I sought the light for the Day of Judgment in generosity (lit. *jud*) and alms-giving (lit. *sakhawah*), but found it in my thirst while fasting. (6) I sought the power of crossing the Bridge (on the Day of Judgment) in sacrifice (of animals, dedicated to Allah), but found it in *sadaqah* (charity). (7) I sought relief from hell-fire in permissible things (lit. *mubah*), but found it in self-control or control of the desires (lit. *shahwah*). (8) I sought love of Allah in worldly things, but found it in His remembrance (lit. *zikr*). (9) I sought happiness in society, but found it in solitude. (10) I sought enrichment of my heart in good advice and (mere) recitation of the Qur'an, but found it in recitation of the Qur'an with humility and tears."

※※※※

In his exegesis of the Qur'anic verse, "And when Ibrahim was tried with certain of commands from his Lord, he fulfilled those in full," Ibn 'Abbas wrote, "Ten practices are amongst the *sunnah* (practices of the Prophet) of which five relate to the head and five to other parts of the body. Those relating to head are: (1) *miswak* (brushing the teeth), (2) rinsing the mouth, (3) washing the nostrils with water, (4) trimming the mustache, and (5) shaving the head. Those of the body parts are: (1) shaving the armpits, (2) cutting nails, (3) shaving pubic hairs, (4) circumcising and (5) cleaning oneself after relieving bowels."

※※※※

Whoever makes *darud*[39] on the Prophet (i.e.,

---

39. Invocation for the Prophet (*s*).

The Counsel

says—peace and blessings of Allah be upon the Prophet) once, Allah blesses that person ten times. On the other hand, whoever speaks ill of him once, Allah curses that person ten times. — Ibn 'Abbas

꙳꙳꙳꙳

Ibrahim bin Adham was questioned why the prayers of people were not granted while Allah says in the Qur'an: "Pray unto Me, and I shall fulfill your prayers". In reply he said, "Your hearts have died because of ten reasons (for which your prayers are not accepted). (These are:) (1) You know Allah, still you do not fulfill His obligations. (2) You read the Qur'an, but still do not follow its instructions. (3) You know that your enemy is Satan, yet you follow him. (4) You claim to love the Messenger of Allah (s), but still you abandon his *sunnah* (ways). (5) You claim to love paradise, but do not do the deeds necessary to inherit such. (6) You claim to fear Hell Fire, but do not refrain from committing sin. (7) You know that death is true, but do not procure the necessary provision for it. (8) You seek the faults of others, but do not look at your own faults. (9) You partake of Allah's sustenance, yet do not thank Him. (10) You lay the dead inside the grave, but do not take lessons there from."

❦❦❦❦

Whoever, man or woman, recites the following *du'a* one thousand times on the night of 'Arafah (i.e., the night before the 'Id al-Adha[40]) and then supplicates Allah to fulfill his or her wish, Allah will not deny that wish as long as it is not for severing relationship with kith or kin or some sinful acts. There are ten sentences in this *du'a*: "Glorified is He Whose Throne is established over the heavens. Glorified is He Whose dominion and power is over the earth. Glorified is He Whose way is in the earth. Glorified is He Whose Spirit permeates the air. Glorified is He Who rules over the fire. Glorified is He Whose knowledge permeates what is in the womb of mothers. Glorified is He Who has control over the graves. Glorified is He Who has raised the sky high without any pillar. Glorified is He Who has spread

---

40. The festival of sacrifice.

The Counsel

out the earth. Glorified is He without Whom there is neither safety nor salvation." — Muhammad (s)

※※※

Ibn 'Abbas related that once the Messenger of Allah (s) asked Iblis (Satan), "Who are your friends amongst my *ummah* (community)?" Iblis replied, "I have friendship with ten types of people. These are: (1) oppressive rulers, (2) those who are proud, (3) rich men who do not discriminate between *halal* (permissible) and *haram* (forbidden) means of their earnings, (4) religious scholars who aid oppressive rulers, (5) dishonest merchants, (6) merchants who hoard in order to raise prices of commodities, (7) adulterers, (8) usurers, (9) misers who earn money illegally and are unconcerned as to how they earn money, and (10) drunkards." Then the Prophet (s) asked him, "Who amongst my *ummah* are your enemies?" Iblis replied, "I have enmity with twenty types of people. (1) The foremost among them is you, O Muhammad. (The others are:) (2) religious scholars whose deeds are in conformity with their knowledge, (3) those who have committed to memory the Qur'an and whose deeds are in conformity with its dictates, (4) callers (lit. *mu'azzin*) for five daily prayers, (5) those who love the poor (lit. *fuqara'*), indigent (lit. *miskin*) and orphans (lit. *yatim*), (6) kind-hearted people, (7) just people, (8) those who spend their youth in obedience of Allah, (9) those who earn *halal* (permissible) livelihood, (10) two young men who love each other for the sake of Allah, (11) those who are particular about praying in gatherings (lit. *jama'ah*) in the mosque, (12) those who wake up at night to worship Allah, (13) those who shun forbidden things, (14) those who offer good advice to others (or pray for others) and their hearts are pure, (15) those who always stay in the state of *wudu'* (ablution), (16) generous people, (17) people of good moral character, (18) those who rely on Allah for everything, (19) those who work for the good of widows, and (20) those who are always prepared for death."

Wahb bin Munabbih said, "In the Torah it is stated—(1) He who earns the provisions for the

The Counsel

Next world in this world will be a dear one to Allah on the Day of Judgment. (2) He who controls his anger will attain proximity to Allah. (3) He who shuns worldly comforts will save himself from Allah's Anger on the Day of Judgment. (4) He who forsakes envy (lit. *hasad*) will be admired by all in the Hereafter. (5) He who gives up the yearning for leadership will be honored by Allah the Almighty, in the Hereafter. (6) He who gives up bounties of this world will find comfort in the Next World. (7) He who shuns quarrels and mischief in this world will earn good repute in the Hereafter. (8) He who gives up miserliness in this world will be admired by all in the Hereafter. (9) He who gives up comfort of this world will be happy in the Hereafter. (10) He who shuns forbidden things in this world will find company amongst the prophets in the Hereafter. (11) He who refrains himself from looking into forbidden things in this world will be blessed with the vision of Allah in Paradise. (12) He who forsakes worldly fortunes to adopt poverty will be raised with the Prophets and friends of Allah on the Day of Judgment. (13) He who helps others in this world will be helped by Allah both in this world and the Next. (14) He who wants to find agreeable companions inside the grave—let him pray at the dead of the night. (15) He who desires the shade underneath the Throne of the Beneficent (i.e., Allah) on the Day of Judgment should shun worldly engagement. (16) He who desires an easy accounting on the Day of Judgment should admonish his soul and those near him with good advice. (17) He who desires encounters with angels in the Next World should resort to piety. (18) He who desires an abode in the middle of Paradise should remember (lit. *zikr*) Allah much night and day. (19) He who wants to be admitted into Paradise should repent sincerely. (20) He wants to be rich should be content with what Allah, the Exalted, has decreed for him. (21) He who wants to be recognized as a jurist (lit. *faqih*) by Allah should be terrified of meeting Him. (22) He who wants to be a judge (lit. *hakim*) should be learned (lit. *'alim*). (23) He who wants to save himself from other's criticism should not criticize others except saying what is good and take lessons by meditating on the purpose behind creation. (24) He who wants to be honored both in this world and the Hereafter should prefer the Next World to this. (25) He who desires peaceful living in the Jannah

The Counsel

al-Firdaws and Jannah al-Na'im (names of two heavens) should save himself from doing corruption (lit. *fasad*) in this world. (26) He who desires a heavenly abode both in this world and the Next should be generous for surely a donor is closer to heaven and faraway from Hell. (27) He who wants to enlighten his heart should resort to inner contemplation all the time. (28) He who wants to restrain his body, engage his tongue with *zikr* and fill his heart with sincerity should seek much forgiveness for all *mu'minun* and Muslims, men and women alike."

Printed in Great Britain
by Amazon

44535471R00088

Thought Fall

The Unfashionable Poet

Published by Steve Singleton, 2025.

Table of Contents

Foreword 1
Example reviewer comments 2
Copyright notice 3
Dedication 4
Street kid - a poem about fate and the dispossessed 5
Group think - a poem about received wisdom 9
Peace - a poem about manipulation 11
Aleppo - a 2016 poem about walking by on the other side 14
Brief encounter - a poem about convergence and divergence 20
Grief - a poem about experiencing loss and hope 23
Fistral - a poem about surf and spirit 26
Passionate - a poem about motivation and recognition 29
Robert - a poem about lessons from a deceased war veteran . 31
The Gulf - a poem about the travel weary and the simply weary 35
Heaven on Earth - a poem about final realisation 38
A life in denim - a poem about wistful memory 42
Beyond the horizon - a poem about population movement .. 44
Planned obsolescence - a poem about a lethal merry go round 49
Our world - a poem about being a victim of invasion 54
Lockdown legacy - a poem about Covid19 lockdown in January 2021 57
The silent message - a poem about mutual dependence 60
After me - a poem about what's important 63
Freedom is not a gift - a poem about priceless privilege 66
Shore road - a poem about memory lane 69
Love - a poem about total immersion 74

Natural connection – a poem about letting life flow 76
Rock, Paper, Scissors – a poem about buffeting and belief 79
Your time – a poem about a unique reign 82
Influencers and influenced - a poem about hidden agendas .. 84
Multi-dimensional - a poem about the tyranny of labels 88
Rewriting history - a poem about cancel culture 92
Just watching - a poem about moral bankruptcy 96
Love is - a poem about personal connection 98
Scorched earth - a poem about blind rage 101
Lifeboat of the lost - a poem about cruising 104
Simply the worst - a poem about award ceremonies 107
What cold? - a poem about chilling detachment 111
Nobody's collateral - a poem about child victims of acquiescence 114
Message to Pasha - a poem about courage and commitment 117
Standing in the rain – a poem about electric vehicles 120
Charity - a poem about loss of focus 127
This boat - a poem about being alive on BM45 130
La Stazione – a poem about a social hub 133
Girl with a dog - a poem about life without limits 136
Common cause – a poem about calling their bluff 139
Behind the façade – a poem about secrets and lies 141
Wrong track – a poem about futile growth 143
Looking down – a poem about a slippery slope 146
Night flight from Singapore - a poem about travel and perspective 149
Clouds of infinity - a poem about the true place of humanity 152
I'm not ready - a poem about perceptions of age 155

Foreword

Poetry has the power to capture and communicate the impact of situations, events and other people on us at a visceral level, when preconceptions are put aside. Some preconceptions stem from the classification of poetry as art, rather than simply high impact communication. The baggage that comes with that can be considerable.

I created The Unfashionable Poet, to write high impact poems that cut through without baggage.

'Thought Fall' is a selection of my poetry covering topics such as Life, War, Love, Loss and Environment, where each poem has follow-on notes regarding the circumstances, motivation and ideas behind it. I hope you will find the book enjoyable and thought-provoking.

Example reviewer comments

"Your poems always make me think, and always bring out strong emotions" - J.A. re 'Brief Encounter' and others in this book

"Thank you for sharing this beautiful poem with me"- M.A. re 'Robert'

"...love the poem, really does set the tone of Fistral.... H.M. re 'Fistral'

"I will pass on your beautifully crafted poem" – R.C. – re 'This Boat

Copyright notice

The contents of this book 'Thought Fall' with my associated nom-de-plume The Unfashionable Poet are the copyright of the author, © The Unfashionable Poet 2025, with all rights strictly reserved. No copying, onward distribution, sale, extracts or re-purposing are permitted without the express and verified written permission of the author.

Further and for the avoidance of doubt, any extract or copying in whole or in part of the contents of this book into any Artificial Intelligence (AI) models, systems or equivalents, or utilisation therein for any purpose, is specifically prohibited

All enquiries should be sent to the author via ssbusenable@gmail.com

Dedication

To Jeanne, who gave me the confidence to be myself

Street kid - a poem about fate and the dispossessed

Sleeping under cardboard
In Mumbai
Shivering on a beach
In Libya
Picking over rubbish tips
In Lagos
Stealing cars, smoking weed
In Leeds
Same look in the eyes
Washed up, but rarely washed
Wasted, like anyone cares
Existing, for today at least
Invisible; so far off piste
Ghosts in plain sight

Meanwhile

The privileged decide what's wrong and right
Those for whom it's no surprise
To be around tomorrow
For another sunrise
Pushing past the begging hand
Everyone a winner
Saving the moment for an amusing dinner
Whatever that is (...)

Street kid – (continued)

Meanwhile

The street kid pauses
Delivering his verdict with his eyes
Knowing; sad for us both
Both losers and winners
Caught in a web of lies
Picking up his World in a bundle
He looks back with pity
We both know, but for fate
It could easily be me
Just another lost soul
In a dog-eat-dog city

Street kid – author's notes

This poem set the tone for much of my other writing, intended to capture life experience and its impact at first hand

It came about as two events coalesced into an idea and a point of view.

I saw the film 'Lion', a true story about the displacement of Saroo, an Indian boy who gets lost on their rail network and spends a long time living rough, destitute and sleeping under the cardboard he carried through the streets of Kolkata, thousands of kilometres from home. The film left a strong impression of the daily realities of his situation and that of other street kids in the city.

Not long afterwards I was a juror in a case of a lad in Yorkshire, who had 'previous' for drug possession and spent nights joy riding with his friends, not necessarily in vehicles they owned.

Street kid – author's notes (continued)

It was not the detail of the case or result that stayed with me, but the sight of his mother bringing clean clothes in for him at lunchtime in a plastic carrier bag, as they awaited the verdict; in case he was convicted and detained. Another street kid with his possessions in a bundle.

Two lost souls among so many.

Group think - a poem about received wisdom

Is what we think
Or what they think
We should think
If we don't think

For ourselves

Group think – author's notes

Probably my shortest poem; but hopefully long enough to make the point

Peace - a poem about manipulation

What is peace?
Is it the absence of war
Or the absence of enemies?
People we are told to hate
Nations, even races
What are foreigners for?

Distractions maybe
From what's actually real
In our daily lives
Of domestic stress
And broken promises
That are part of the deal

All while political failures
Spouting strategy
Whistle stop the world
In kings new clothes
And government jets
To perpetuate tragedy

Fuelled by billions
Thrown at 'defence'
As nations square off
And costs magically double
In our lives and treasure
All this makes no sense (...)

Peace – (continued)

Except to arms companies
And the threats they contrive
Putting 'leaders' in their pockets
Who play human chess
While we are shot or starve
But they always survive

As if we didn't notice

Peace – author's notes

I was thinking

What is peace when we spend so much time and effort preparing for war? Time, money, pre-occupation, stereotyping, orchestrated anger; anything but the tranquillity of peace.

Are we like rats competing in a crowded maze, or are we more intelligent than that? Perhaps those who have most to gain are cunning enough to take the thinking off of our hands; keeping us off balance while leveraging conflict to distract from what they are doing or not delivering elsewhere.

We need to wake up, decide and take control of what peace is for. Because it needs to be more than a waiting room for war.

That thought is the foundation of 'Peace'.

Aleppo - a 2016 poem about walking by on the other side

In the ruins of civilisation
Morals die, children cry
Bathed in chlorine
Screaming forlornly
In bombed out basements
As we watch 'Strictly'

They have no options
Living a nightmare
With no food, no charity
No succour or safe exit
As we sit on our hands
And witter about Brexit

We have choices
They do not have
We can scream enough!
We can prioritise
Face our shame
Through Christ's eyes (...)

Aleppo – (continued)

Nothing matters more
Than the innocents
Trapped in this hell
It's down to all of us
Not to pass by
On the road to Damascus

Forget exchange rates
Forget holiday plans
Forget gadgets
Forget fashion
Nights on the town
Or other selfish passions

This is what happens
When the thin crust crumbles
Make no mistake
As the Manic Street Preachers predicted
If you tolerate this
Ignore the lost and afflicted

Then your children will be next

Aleppo – author's notes

A number of my poems reflect my feelings of guilt at living safe and free, while whole populations are jeopardised by war.

'Aleppo' is one of my earliest war poems, prompted by the horrors of Assad's forces barrel bombing civilians in the city; including use of chlorine that had to be desperately washed off children by floods of water as they screamed. Where there was water available......

I felt the contrast between many of us being comfortable watching our favourite television programmes at home while Aleppo's children were dying and being horribly maimed was important to highlight.

At the time I was moved enough to send this poem to government ministers and even the United Nations; to be met by......silence. God knows what they thought was more important at the time.

Bucha - a poem about war crimes

We are cold now
But that is not new
No longer hungry though
No longer angry
Or frantic
Without a clue
How to get out of here
Alive

We are deaf now
To the echoes of our babies cries
We wiped dust from their mouths
Held them close
To shield them
From seeing death
In all its flavours
Raining from the skies

Or maybe that boy there
Who's not much older
Than my son
The assault rifle
Shaking in his hand
As the blank imperatives of fear
Pull his trigger
To follow Putin's order (...)

Bucha – (continued)

We are frozen now
Beyond the chill of fear
When we were tied
No expectation
Of mercy
Or deliverance then
No way back
We would not be leaving here

Except to be buried
In Bucha

Bucha – author's notes

'Bucha' is a contemporaneous war poem, spawned by television images of early atrocities in the Russian invasion of Ukraine.

It was hard to ignore half buried corpses of civilians, shot with hands tied behind their back in the ruins of their homes in this town. I wanted to give them a voice, while attempting to share the individual horrors of their doom; often executed at the hands of flaky young Russian conscripts.

With the spotlight currently trained on the obscene genocides of the middle east, it would be too easy to forget these slaughtered pawns in Putin's game.

There is no normalising of cold-blooded murder, whatever the context.

Brief encounter - a poem about convergence and divergence

February
It's cold
A biting Easterly
Snow flurries in the air
Here
At a petrol station
On a low hill
In the middle of nowhere
South-west of Reims
Just you and me
Initially
Until that noise
A shrieking symphony
Descends through serial blips
Crackling overrun
Until there he was
Coasting to a stop
A vision in Ray-bans
And race boots
Sliding out of that car
An object of envy
A low sleek Ferrari
In Sunday best scarlet
Naturally
But he did not have the girl
Brave and beautiful like you (...)

Brief encounter – (continued)

Beside me
On our last adventure
In our relatively humble BMW
Although you were dying
Although I was smiling
My eyes said I was lying
Then the Ferrari was gone
Disappearing like an arrow
Towards the horizon
It was time to push on
To our own destination
Venice
A dream no longer
For our remaining time together
And I will always remember
Always

Brief encounter – author's notes

There are road trips and there are road trips.

Who takes it into their head to drive from the U.K. to Venice across the Alps in the middle of winter? Unless they have a very special reason.

The brief encounter with the Ferrari, on a bleak day in the middle of nowhere, was both poignant and surreal; during a bucket list trip for someone very close to me, who was not well enough to fly.

We made it to Venice a few days later after our share of adventures en route.

She died 6 months after the trip.

Grief - a poem about experiencing loss and hope

This alien situation
Is outside your experience
But the hurt is real enough
Whether fast or slow
A hammer blow,
In a velvet glove of dulled senses
Untouched by well-meaning phrases
Or denial against the cold steel of reality
A bad dream that you don't want to share
Which hits you in waves of fear
Realisation and detachment
From those who care
About you

But you are not you
Not whole as before
Now something different
In a pit
Without your reason for living
And no clue how to handle it
Crying inconsolably
Mostly secretly
Putting on a front
God knows how
While wanting to run
Somewhere, anywhere (...)

Grief – (continued)

That is not here or now
Lost; between the past
And whatever awaits
How could this be?
What used to be us
Only yesterday
Is now only me
Until much later
You may realise
You still have a choice
The future is calling
And the laugh in her voice
Is a message

A miraculous invitation
To shared salvation
If you are listening

Grief – author's notes

While I can only imagine the chaotic and terrifying experience of being under fire in a war, I do not have to imagine deep personal loss.

When my wife died, even though it had coming for some time, I was in a dark and isolated place. Not that others did not try to help, but those that have been there know how impenetrable and shocking grief can be. Before you know it, even friends have checked out and you are truly alone.

Anyone who finds salvation from this loss of identity and hope is lucky and we are all different.

I wrote 'Grief' to try to transmit the lasting impact from the inside, not just for myself. Hopefully this will help other sufferers just a little.

Fistral - a poem about surf and spirit

The roar, that familiar roar
Then the hiss of the waves
Streaking up the beach
Cleaning out the tourists
On their body boards
Like washed up seal pups

As

Having done their thing
Carving the face, further out
The pros can't wait
To return to the line
Stalling their short boards
Into stylish pull ups

While (...)

Fistral – (continued)

I stand on the edge
As I have many times
Important times, in my life
Letting Fistral wash over me
Looking for clarity
On my options

So

It's time to get in
Push the board out again
Turning into the swell
Giving into the rush
A case of needs must
As I chase solutions

Once more

Fistral – author's notes

Many of us have a special place, somewhere that resonates at different points in our lives, drawing us back.

Fistral beach in Cornwall is now a favourite destination for the Range Rover set; complete with fashion outlets, beach bar decking and posh fish and chips, but none of this detracts from the draw of the Atlantic surf pounding the shore there.

When I first went it was just sand dunes and the landmark red brick hotel on the northern headland. I visited with my family often, then alone after bereavement and with my second wife since. We had probably passed in the hotel lift or restaurant over the years as we both took our families there for the Spring bank holiday week, yet strangely our first hello happened much later and 4,500 miles away. Fate I guess, but Fistral has always been there when needed.

Passionate - a poem about motivation and recognition

Passionate,
In everything I think
Everything I do
Because I want to
Because I need to
Because everything else is short-change
Because I know no other way
Because I am all or nothing
Because I want to improve things
Because I want to improve everything
For everyone
Because it's what I do
Because it's how I am
Because it's all I know
Because I doubt myself
Because in a bloody world
Full of bloodless people
Passion matters
And that is what I see
That is what I love
That is what I cherish
Most of all
About you

Passionate – author's notes

A runaway train of a poem; reflecting unrestrained and undisguised emotion

Why? Because sometimes our motivation is not obvious, even to those closest to us. Sometimes you just have to step up, step out and just say it; say what you mean and say what they mean to you. I have sometimes made the mistake of not doing that and other times I have overdone it.

So I wrote 'Passionate' for my wife, to blow away misunderstanding.

Robert - a poem about lessons from a deceased war veteran

They told me you died tonight

It was the World's loss, for those in the know
For those who care about how we got here
From there, that place experienced in black and white
When the whole World was on edge, on the brink
With no future worth the name
Until people like you stood up
In your millions
With every day existential,
With every battle resisting the end of time

Friends perished; others survived to tell the tale
To those who could listen; much later
Having seen the movie, knowing it all
Or so they thought
Not living the nightmares
Not hearing the voices of lost mates
Bearing witness every day
While life goes on, as it does
Because you all made that possible (...)

Robert – (continued)

And you were part of the new dawn
Lessons hopefully learned
Striving for traction in a brave New World
Not counted amongst the graspers; the cynical
Emerging from their bunkers
Regaining control of their normality
Once the niceties had been observed
Once real heroes had marched by
On their one day in the Sun

You became Mum's Husband, our Dad, our Grandad
Hard working, quietly funny, with no inside track
Ambitious only for the things that matter
Making our futures so much better
While carrying a silent burden; made worse by later loss
Sometimes put upon, but never counting the cost
And it's not over; your legacy will last
We will live our futures remembering lessons
You retold from your past

Robert – author's notes

Three young men caught up in war together, none more than 18 years old.

One would not survive, but my father was one of the two that did: so he told me eventually, when he was 85.

I had always wondered why my father used his middle name, until he told me Robert was the one that was killed as their bren gun carrier was blown over a wall by a near miss from a German tank shell in Italy; so my father 'retired' his own first name of Robert after that, out of respect.

Very typical of him.

As we talked I learned more about his quiet bravery, survivors guilt and the difficulty many war fighters had returning to a society where some had prospered in their absence, while they had to start from scratch with their only acquired skill being combat

Robert – author's notes (continued)

So 'Robert' is a testimony to my father and all those that have known the ice-cold fear and existential threats of battle.

For us.

The Gulf - a poem about the travel weary and the simply weary

2:00 AM

This blinding terminal is full of the listless
From who knows where, going everywhere
Looking for an identity, seeking novelty
Driven to find meaning in the meaningless

The gap year student in baggy clothes
Heading East for 'The Triangle' and Kathmandu
Locked into social media, reporting every move
Quietly desperate that everyone knows

The ageing surfer in cut-off jeans
Heading South-East for Padang Padang and Cloud 9
Sponsors had moved on, so he was too
On the last ride of his dreams (...)

The Gulf – (continued)

The boomer couple reliving the past they never had
Heading South to Bondi and Milford Sound
Head to toe in Boden and Berghaus
Life in their version of the Sixties was not so bad

The volunteer on a mercy mission
Heading South-West to save Africa
Full of zeal and Christian hope
Expecting the natives would share her vision

The oilman in a crumpled suit
Heading West to the latest action
No amount of money seemed enough
Whether it bought him happiness was strictly moot

4:00 AM

All gone, all quiet in the hall
The privileged on their way
The poor left to sweep the floor
Shaking their heads and whispering about the unfairness of it all

The Gulf – author's notes

Do you like airports? They may be wearisome but they are people watching opportunities on steroids, particularly at the large international hubs.

If you are travelling east long haul you are quite likely to change planes at some brightly lit middle east terminal in the middle of the night. Slumped in a seat, half asleep and watching travellers from all over the world pass through.

I have been there and the characters in 'The Gulf' have all been encountered over the years. Privileged examples, like me, of humans on the move with their different reasons to travel.

Meanwhile, invisible people clean up around and behind them.

Heaven on Earth - a poem about final realisation

What if here was heaven?
Whatever your divinity
This is it
That's your lot
All there is
In this arm of the galaxy

What if here was heaven?
Walking undisturbed on a beach
Waves tumbling
Sand hissing
Seabirds crying
All your troubles out of reach

What if here was heaven?
Dining raucously with friends
Lost in laughter
Wondrous vistas
New-found lovers
Who knows where this ends? (...)

Heaven on Earth – (continued)

What if here was heaven?
Watching wildlife on the plain
Fluid movements
Sudden drama
Fireball sunsets
Snuffed out like a flame

What if here was heaven?
Seas of flowers
Senses swamped
Just wandering
Thoughts floating free
Feeling empowered

What if here was heaven?
With your partner
Through thick and thin
Lose or win
Rich or poor
Who could want more? (...)

Heaven on Earth – (continued)

Except us
Animals with pretensions
And unfettered greed
Laying waste
To our heavenly home
Fuelled by dumb ambitions

So if earth is heaven
With no hereinafter
This dumb acquiescence
This blown inheritance
Requiring divine salvation
Ends in certain disaster

As God is now busy

Elsewhere

Heaven on Earth – author's notes

It seems our amazing planet is a rarity in the galaxy. Even if it wasn't, humans are not leaving en masse anytime soon.

But what if this was really it, Earth our only roll of the dice, whether by random chance or our ration of divine intervention?

The idea for 'Heaven on Earth' came to me as I reflected on the wonders of our world and the basis of our expectations of heaven.

So here we are. If Earth is our ration of heaven we had best not waste it.

A life in denim - a poem about wistful memory

A fading chord from a forgotten guitar
Dust settles on a track to nowhere
A discarded boot at the end of the boardwalk
By a rusting Harley
Frame the dreams you had
Back then
When everything was future
Your hair not lank and grey
The Sun bright, like her eyes
Waves that picked you up
Rather than dump you on the shore
In a heap
You had options
If you ever thought that way
Over the music in your head
An album from the Grateful Dead
Love and protest
Spliff and truth
Or so you thought
With all the innocence of youth
Remembered

A life in denim – author's notes

This poem is a blend of personal experience and aspiration. Easy Rider imagery merged with real life adventures freewheeling in California.

But we all age.

Glastonbury has replaced Woodstock in rock legend, while born again bikers can no longer carve that perfect curve, now more likely to lean on Ibuprofen than highway 1, while sandy locks become simply grey.

Still there is life in those eyes, even defiance, as wistful memories linger through a paisley filter. 'A life in denim' was inspired by a moment of reflection, contrasting life now with an exciting and non-conformist but fast receding time.

Beyond the horizon - a poem about population movement

People always flow
In the same direction as money
Whether commuting to London
Fleeing war or climate collapse
Why wouldn't you gravitate
Towards the milk and honey?

In a world of flux

Why live just to survive?
It's all there to be seen
A better life you can touch
In high definition
Via the window
Of a smartphone screen

Even if doing nothing is an option (...)

Beyond the horizon – (continued)

Why stay put?
When you don't have to
Crossing deserts by Hilux
That even Clarkson couldn't break
It's survival of the fittest
So why not you?

With nothing to lose

Except an imposed slot
Within the status quo
Strictly 'third world'
And exploited of course
But until recent awakening
Whose was to know?

As if that's an excuse

But it's over
Simply unsustainable
Such inequality has no case
With no basis for entitlement
In a world getting smaller
Migration is not containable (...)

Beyond the horizon – (continued)

A hard fact we must face

People will continue
To follow the money
Until resources
And conditions are shared
They will not stay put
Just to keep others happy

And nor would we

So if our only answer
Is to throw up a wall
To keep things as they were
Beyond the horizon
Then wars will result
And our empires will fall

Inevitably

Beyond the horizon – author's notes

I often ponder inequality, as much from the opportunity and family sustainability perspective as the moral case. Bad things happen when inequality is endemic and not just for those at the bottom of the pecking order. Everything from famine to global pandemics and wars, impacting us all.

Trying to put yourself in the shoes of the disadvantaged can be difficult, but it is the key to informed problem and solution analysis. So imagine you and your family are at the bottom of the heap, far from safety and relative prosperity. What would you do?

In times past you might be ignorant of what you were missing out on, but smartphones put paid to that. Or immobile, but local availability of more reliable minivans, pickup trucks and boats put paid to that. Or suppressed by dominant outside forces, but social networks and asymmetric war capabilities are putting paid to that.

Beyond the horizon – author's notes – (continued)

So here you are, informed, mobile and determined. Why would you not follow the trail to a better life? For as long as there is a money (aka prosperity) gradient you would be dumb to ignore it. Mass and uncontrolled migration are then inevitable and unstoppable on current terms. Unless of course development, resources and prosperity are shared and the gradient starts to level off.

However, it seems we would rather try to defend the moat and build walls than resolve problems in the source regions. Rather have corruption, territorial wars and strip underdeveloped lands of their resources than face up to the inevitable.

'Beyond the horizon' was written to highlight reasons why that is a doomed strategy.

Planned obsolescence - a poem about a lethal merry go round

A B21 bomber costs $700m
So let's have a 100
Shall we? oh yes
We can't take on China
With anything less

An F35 is a snip
At a mere $80m
So let's have a job lot
As they're undetectable
But actually they're not

Still, no problem
As the next big thing.
The F47, is more stealthy
Although at $300m each
The budget needs to be healthy

Not that China abstains
Or Russia come to that
With a fleet of new ships
And hypersonic missiles
They can shoot from the hip (...)

Planned obsolescence – (continued)

And for what?
To fight the next war
Just as night follows day
Never mind mere civilians
Who might get in the way

This sort of investment
Demands a bloody return
A substantial dividend
From a merry go round
That's unlikely to end

Weapons breed conflict
Enable wars
By their presence
And we are the victims
Of this planned obsolescence

Planned obsolescence – author's notes

Defence is an interesting word, especially when an enemy can strike anywhere on the planet, with precision, in a fraction of a day. So now 'first strike' (aka 'getting your retaliation in first') is becoming non optional if you want to have any capability left to defend with.

Of course you have to counter that first strike if you can, at ever longer range, while the attackers need ever more sophistication to get through. 'Twas ever thus' but now we are approaching the point where every advance costs many $Billions with a single bomber the best part of $1Billion to deploy, while people still starve.

'Planned obsolescence' highlights the absurdity of what we have become too used to; where familiarity clouds an insidious threat and arms industry employment levels seem to outweigh sanity. This distortion of reality has the potential to make both 'defence' and humanity obsolete.

Butterfly blizzard - a poem about predatory deception

Looks like a blizzard of butterflies here today
Wounded butterflies
Fluttering from an azure sky
Onto the waste ground where the children play
Carrying false promises of safety if you leave your home
But then if you choose to stay you'll be on your own
When 'top guns' dispassionately pull the trigger
And the holes all around you just get bigger
Filling with the bodies of family and friends, labelled human shields
As if that's an excuse
Since there's nowhere to run to, from these killing fields
And as those who can run no more draw their last breath
Those butterflies are revealed as harbingers of death

Butterfly blizzard – author's notes

Imagine being there. A gorgeous blue sky filled with small, falling and tumbling white shapes.

Even children have learned what this blizzard means.

'Invited' to leave your fragile refuge by these lethal leaflets you have no safe place to go, or any way to get anywhere that does not involve risking death for you and your remaining family en route; as all sorts of lethal munitions burst through the man-made cloud to consign you to agony or oblivion.

'Butterfly Blizzard' is one a series written from the perspective of those some refer to as 'collateral damage' or 'human shields'. Convenient labels for the orphans of our conscience.

Our world - a poem about being a victim of invasion

Is the next minute
Next hour
Next night
Next bullet
Next bomb
Next rocket
Next drink
Next crust
Next dash
For cover
For hospital
For life

Who knows when
We will see our children
Mother
Husband
Partner
Or wife?
Lives out of control
In a blasted basement
Under rubble
In smoking ruins
That were once
Kharkiv or Mariupol (...)

Our world – (continued)

This is our world
A fading echo
It seems
In the global context
Inconveniently stubborn
For those in the West
Countries untouched
In the 'defence of freedom'
Happy hours
Happy families
Happy holidays
Except it's your turn next

Our world – author's notes

It is not easy to capture the threat, panic, pace, chaos and jeopardy of being victims of war in the written word. The Ukraine war has brutally highlighted this, but the challenge exists in every shooting conflict.

It is one thing to contemplate and try to articulate war from a distance, for example through television news and documentaries, quite another to be there and experience it in the first person.

'Our world' is one of several attempts I have made to truly put the reader in the victim's shoes, with the chaotic and escalating impact of their extraordinary situation.

Lockdown legacy - a poem about Covid19 lockdown in January 2021

Quiet

Quiet everywhere
No cars, at least very few
Except for 4x4s
Complete families
Escaping to the country
With cases of Chablis
Was that you?

Quiet everywhere
No planes, that you can see
Except for private jets
'Celebrities' cocooned
While we're all marooned
Not fazed by rules
That "don't apply to me"

Quiet everywhere
Nothing in the country
Except for wildlife
Coming out of cover
Drowned out for so long
The loudest sound is birdsong
As it always should be (...)

Lockdown legacy – (continued)

Quiet everywhere
No one in the pubs
Except for the landlords
Waiting and wondering
Is this the end?
Will this business ever mend?
As everyone's hub

Quiet everywhere
Where could this go?
How much can we stand?
People in fear
Will it be safe anytime this year?
Or have we lost our nerve?
Nobody knows

Quiet
Quiet everywhere
Except in our minds

Lockdown legacy – author's notes

Lockdown Legacy' was written in the depths of the Covid pandemic; a surreal and threatening time that affected us all. It was best done then, when emotions were raw and before some of us started to wonder if that jarring interruption to our lives had really happened.

I was attempting to capture the in the moment impacts and uncertainties, shared by most and avoided by some, while also reflecting the early signs of legacy effects.

For all its high drama and controversies that period was a test of the resilience of our world. Perhaps this poem will help later generations to have some appreciation of what is was like on the inside.

The silent message - a poem about mutual dependence

Today, the silence is deafening
As deafening as shellfire
Birdsong on mute
Marshlands poisoned
Wheatfields a lethal quagmire
Flyways filled with missiles
Where what was beautiful
Is obliterated by the mechanical

Today, the golden thread
Of mutual dependence is broken
From Bucha to Kharkiv
And hamlets in between
No place to call home
Where the rhythm of nature
Is strictly for the birds
Now flown, and rarely seen

Today, migrating bean geese
Have few places left to rest
Demoiselle cranes fly on
Like waders and songbirds
With no safe sites to nest
Each one evicted from their range
And all but disappearing
From their strongholds in Ukraine (...)

The silent message – (continued)

One day, God willing
Best not left to man
The cranes could return
To marshes cleansed of war
Long legged buzzards scavenge
On more than human remains
Bustards strut fields free of mines
Scattered for marginal gains

At no time was this small world
Ours to waste and throw away
We need to heed the message
From Ukraine's steppes today
Mindless habitat destruction
Without sane reason or pretext
Where the birds know what bad looks like
And it looks like our turn next

The silent message – author's notes

War is a massive pollution event, at every level.

From the material destruction to vast tracts of land laid to waste and scattered with lethal debris, destroying the environment for living things deep into the future.

And we are not the only living things.

The steppes and river deltas of Ukraine are not just battlefields but vital wildlife habitats and bird migration routes of global significance. And they are being devastated, leaving a persistent and poisonous legacy. 'Silent message' was written as a wake-up call; highlighting a critical situation where the obliteration of wildlife and the environment herald our own destruction.

After me - a poem about what's important

There will still be children
Innocent for as long as allowed
Optimistic, everything a wonder
Everything possible
In their dreams

There will still be rivers
Some meandering through meadows
Carpeted in mayfly
Some thundering through gorges
Meltwater from a thousand streams

There will still be mothers
Doing their best
Committed
Taking a qualified risk
On the future

There will still be forests
Patient sentinels
Waiting for us
To come to our senses
Like intelligent creatures (...)

After me – (continued)

There will still be fathers
Faithful or absentee
Daunted, feigning confidence
Rebels no longer
Without the option

There will still be oceans
Rolling forward, cresting
Breaking the horizon
Where albatross glide endlessly
On their circumnavigation

There will still be a whisper
An eddy of my presence
As the world moves on
My love for you immortal
My life's best decision

All that mattered, in the end

After me – author's notes

All of us are just passing through as the world, in some form, moves forward. As I get older I think more about the interplay of individuals and relationships with that continuum.

What will we leave behind, or do we just live in the moment, preferably mindfully?

'After me' was written with those questions in mind.

And the conclusion? Relationships and the stories they leave behind define your legacy, your imprint on the world.

It is our golden thread.

Freedom is not a gift - a poem about priceless privilege

Even if it's your norm
Waking up in bed
Loving the one you choose
Having plans for the weekend
Chillaxing
Or relaxing to those with no metro
Who shall I see?
What will we discuss?
What will I buy?
All these decisions
That will depend
On where you were born

Or when
When we were top dog
Our God given right
To live in the moment
Doing the least
To get the most
No scratching around
Like those on the new
With their daily agony
Until we wake up to a nightmare
With the good times a memory
Where now is not then (...)

Freedom is not a gift – (continued)

It takes more than an expresso
To give us a lift
As it finally dawns
That freedom is not a gift

Freedom is not a gift – author's notes

This poem was created to address the sort of complacency and entitled expectation that pass for the natural order of things with many

Life can be comfortable for us today, enjoying freedoms and prosperity largely won by others.

But there are seismic changes around the corner, as tyrants, technology, population and climate change effectively shrink the world.

'Freedom is not a gift' poses a question. How prepared are we for the freedoms we take for granted to be challenged, or perhaps just stop?

Shore road - a poem about memory lane

Shore road
Is just a dead-end street
A sandy lane
Past a jazz cafe
Where dog walkers meet

But I have loved it

Man and boy
Such great memories there
Off the open top bus
Holding my father's hand
Endless days without care

And we were not rich

Before blue glass and chrome
There was no need to be
As we roamed around Sandbanks
With our view of the water
Uninterrupted and free (...)

Shore road – (continued)

Like my father before

And his father too
Digging cockles for tea
Having fought in both wars
To return to these shores
They were heroes to me

Then much later

Being one of the lads
Girlfriend riding pillion
On my sporty Honda
With her Mary Quant hair
Looking one in a million

And later still

With you
The stunning love of my life
And the dog came too
As I nearly blew asking
If you would be my wife (...)

Shore road – (continued)

So shore road is special

So much more
Than just a dead-end street
Down the lane
Past the cafe
Is where life and dreams meet

Shore road – author's notes

Those who know Poole in Dorset, or perhaps Harry Redknapp, know shore road as the east end of the Sandbanks peninsula, sometime most expensive residential land in the world, apparently.

But locals from the wrong side of the tracks, like me, have different memories; experienced more than half a century ago and at important times since. We may not be millionaires but we can at least afford the car park fee.

So shore road is a temporal crossroads for me, bearing the footprints of my grandparents, parents, siblings, cousins, school friends, girlfriends, wives and children. Standing there I can recall them still. Turning round I half expect to see them there, as if in a dream.

Shore road – author's notes (continued)

But time waits for no-one. Shore road has moved on and so have I.

This poem looks to walk the reader in my footprints, in one of my happy places, before they are washed away for ever.

Love - a poem about total immersion

Is not so much felt
As lived
In every corner of your mind
In every moment
A pulse
Setting the rhythm
The context
Of being
Who you are
Where you both exist
In each other's world
A world more focused
Yet liberated
Bigger
Boundless
Fast
Yet savouring
Each second
In slow time
Like a car crash
Of emotions
Overwhelming
All senses
Without limit

This is it

Love – author's notes

Much poetry is observational but can struggle to be experiential.

'Love' is another poem where I look to capture the rush of life on fast forward from the inside, accelerating towards a hopefully thought-provoking takeaway.

Natural connection – a poem about letting life flow

Right here
There's no sound
But the last surge
Of a wave
Onto the shore
Like glass beads
Thrown across a marble floor
Washing around our ankles
My thoughts float free
Going with the flow
As it recedes now
With a hiss
To the enveloping sea

Right now
There's no urgency
As the ocean breeze
Cools my skin
Slows down time
Time to discover
What's important to me
When there's nothing to prove
A rare moment of silence
I just need this space
With a quiet mind (...)

Natural connection – (continued)

Outside the envelope
Exploring the ways
For my life to recover

Right place
There's no doubt
To capture that feeling
A sense of belief
In living off script
Outside the cacophony
With everything possible
And no need to conform
To give decisions validity
It's time to give pause
Where we stand on this beach
As it's now crystal clear
That you are the one
And those dreams are in reach

Natural connection – author's notes

'Natural Connection' is about recognising and seizing the moment in a personal relationship

A moment happening in a favourite place where routine existence takes a back seat and time slows down, before going fast forward on the other side

Nothing clinical or calculated, just risk and instinct. A moment of consequence at a temporal crossroads

Before she said yes.

Rock, Paper, Scissors – a poem about buffeting and belief

I've seen you happy

With the laugh that stops time,
A smile that completely disarms
A touch that both calms and electrifies
A whisper that roars through my head
My instinct to reach out
Envelop and keep you from harm

I've seen you shattered

A cry of pain that cut me in two
Events that challenged all you were
Your energy, positivity and nurturing core
We came through all that
Maybe not unscathed
But sustained by what we are

You've seen me ecstatic (...)

Rock, Paper, Scissors – (continued)

Rescued from the brink
By your miracle
Out of a clear blue sky
A direction other than down
Shared instinct replacing despair
Altered perceptions of what is possible

You've seen me depressed

Illogical, unfair, demonstrably stupid
Angst that risks self – fulfilment
Fretting about nothing and everything
Haunted by historic insecurity
Lashing out while caving in
Words and reactions that were never meant

But we are strong

As we always have been
Right from the beginning
Speaking softly, holding on
With love and patience
Belief in our future, cutting through
Knowing we enrich each other's being

Rock, Paper, Scissors – author's notes

This is a poem about the mental health side of relationships. Not all hearts and flowers, through thick and thin.

I was moved to write it through a particularly stressful period, where our core support for and belief in each other was never more important.

Just like the Rock, Paper, Scissors game, we did not know what would come next.

Life in the raw, but a positive message overall.

Your time – a poem about a unique reign

If it is near the end
As even the almighty cannot amend
You will be missed
By all of us
Who shared your time
And others
Who may not appreciate it yet
Latter day cynics
Who did not know then
So cannot understand
Your service
To all of us
For 70 years
And if there are tears
Let them be of pride
That we are ready
Ready now
For whenever
We have to manage
Without you
At our side

Your time – author's notes

Queen Elizabeth the second was an ever present in my life and that of my family, until she died in September 2022. She performed a role from a young age that many might covet, but only a handful have done well down the centuries, with professionalism and grace.

'Your time' was written as her health faded, four months before her death, as we came to terms with the reality that her remaining time was short.

There were many obituaries and eulogies written later, some better grounded in every-day language than others. This is mine.

Influencers and influenced - a poem about hidden agendas

Why do we need to be told?

What's good
Or good for us
What's cool
Or on trend
What's hot
Or not
What's truth
Or lies
Should we not realise

Why do we need influencers?

Who are nothing new
Whose success depends
On creating disciples
Not usually so rash
Who pass on the message
Without thinking
Or pausing to notice
How influencers benefit
Via control or cash (...)

Influencers and influenced – (continued)

So where does it stop?

In this pyramid sell
Followers recruit more
A captive audience
Needing to belong
To whatever this might be
As valuable commodities
Subscribers to the cause
Bought into the message
Whether right or wrong

So where could this go?

A world of 'experts'
Who know better
Or at least a good thing
Distracting from what's real
To their advantage
Some leveraging preconceptions
And prejudice
While many of us
Are asleep at the wheel
So wake up

Influencers and influenced – author's notes

I guess there have always been influencers and leaders with followers e.g. in tribes, nations, politics and religion

Historically they would have to demonstrate their strength and the merits of their direction consistently, along with some practical benefits for followers within their local sphere of influence. Give or take a Pied Piper of Hamlin their target audience was adults.

Now, access to the internet via smart mobile phones means that any influencer can reach any person, of any age and maturity, at any time, across the globe and in private, which has consequences.

Influencers and influenced – author's notes (continued)

Having observed the reach of many self-serving self-publicists promoting ideas, products and services that range from fake news to fragile and fake consumer offerings, while making money regardless through follower count, I felt motivated to write 'Influencers and influenced'.

The poem is suggesting it's time to stop feeding this monster in our pockets and think for ourselves again

Multi-dimensional - a poem about the tyranny of labels

Are you
Conservative, Liberal
Or Socialist
Black or Brown
White or Other
Old, Young
Or in between
Christian, Muslim
Or Atheist?

Are you
Boxed and labelled
Captured by some survey
Or so they think
Predictable
Within your cohort
Influenceable
To see things
Their way? (...)

Multi-dimensional – (continued)

Or are we more
Than one dimensional
A mere classification
Being a unique blend
Of complex experience
And perspectives
Unbounded
Thinking as individuals
About every situation?

Multi-dimensional – author's notes

Are you fed up with questionnaires?
Whether market survey or opinion poll, there are analysts with a need to demonstrate that they understand you, what influences you and your opinions, while never having met you. Real people and their views are not so easy to capture; despite the claims of companies that seem to melt away when challenged to predict election landslides, let alone tight contests, or to excuse regular marketing disasters based on their conclusions.
Are they all dumb? No, but sometimes you need to stand in the bus queue, sit in the pub, be on the production line, just listening. Opinion formers do not sit exclusively in glass towers or inside the M25, while public mood shifts can materialise before 'insiders' have a clue.

Multi-dimensional – author's notes

'Multi-dimensional' was written with this in mind. Human beings are gloriously individual and still reveal most about what they are thinking when face to face, with people they trust.
Long may it continue.

Rewriting history - a poem about cancel culture

Because history is complex
Facts inconvenient
The truth is immutable
Slave trading was universal
From Rome to Greece
Africa and Arabia
England and America
Europe and Asia
Shameful everywhere
Of the past
Yet still there
Not unique
Nothing singular
To fuel latter day pique
About monuments to cruelty
Which is a global reality
That we cannot deny
Or erase from our memory
While repeating the error
Of allowing factional pressure
To cancel the truth
Rather than face it
And own it
Learn lessons together
From the abuse (...)

Rewriting history – (continued)

Rather than bully
Other people
With violent invective
To submit like slaves
To our narrow perspective

Rewriting history – author's notes

This process has always happened and will continue to happen. They say that victors get to write history, but being top dog is cyclical, so even that is malleable. Who has the ultimate truth? All we can do is attempt to ensure we have as complete a perspective as possible, without fear or favour. But we rarely seem to do that.

Hijacking of a single threaded version of the past to gain current advantage, rather than apply lessons to improve the future for all, is currently fashionable, going on sinister.

As an example, slavery in any form or era is abhorrent and indefensible. It is very common throughout human history, including World War 2 and currently, which excuses nothing and nobody; whatever their state of development or knowledge at the time. No region or nation has had a monopoly on this sin.

Rewriting history – author's notes (continued)

Rewriting history' looks to highlight this challenge, while suggesting that erasure of an inconvenient past is equally unproductive.

Just watching - a poem about moral bankruptcy

A distant thud, the air ripped like fabric
The terminal rush and shriek of arriving munitions
Before the world dissolves into thunder,
Shattered glass, falling masonry and choking dust
As the sky disappears
Before the obscene aftermath of screams
The agony of the lost and the dying
Father! ……mother!……children!
I cannot see! …..I cannot feel!
I am burning!
Then silence, a temporary silence
Except for scattered papers
Fluttering, personal, but private no longer
Before the low moans of departing souls
The bottomless pits of bereavement
The terror, the waste
The terrible, endless, senseless waste
Of people, real people, babies
Thousands of innocents
On both sides of the line
For nothing, simply nothing
That will stand the test of time

And we just watch?

Just watching – author's notes

'Just watching' reflects my desire, need really, to communicate the visceral experiences of innocent people under fire, from their perspective. An attempt to rip the curtain and remove the detachment of those of us observing from a safe distance; while highlighting the waste, the permanent waste, of war.

Also, to reinforce that the savagery of bombardment of civilians should never be normalised; seen as any more acceptable than the prototypical bombing of Guernica in 1937, illustrated and communicated so starkly by Picasso.

Often we absorb such slaughter passively, passing by on the other side; presumably hoping there will be no day of judgement

Love is - a poem about personal connection

Complicated
Indefinable
In a world addicted
To definitions
Precision
Classifications and comparisons
Rules
Other people's rules
Framing what's ordinary
But this isn't
This is different

This is our world
Exclusive
Electric
Involving
Exciting
Unrestrained
Hot
Yet calm
Reflective
Unlocking the future
Like never before (...)

Love is – (continued)

A new world
Because it's our time
Because we want it
Because we live it
And we just know

Love is – author's notes

Love is better experienced and felt than verbalised; where it is difficult to avoid cliches.

This poem attempts to step inside the bubble of a freshly connected couple, to the exclusion of the limits and norms of everyday existence. It also reflects the need to recognise 'the one', take a chance and seize the moment; or regret it forever.

And yes, it was written during the extraordinary whirlwind of a new romance.

Scorched earth - a poem about blind rage

It's a war of annihilation
Erasing neighbours and neighbourhoods
As final solutions return
And children burn
In the rubble of their future

With tit for tat retaliation
No matter innocents in the way
There's no moral high ground
And no victory to be found
In such nihilistic culture

And no chance of negotiation
Until the warmongering stops
Along with the bloodletting
Which we can't be forgetting
In the foreseeable

It's such a cold calculation
Ends justifying means
In a uniformed mind
Where vengeance is blind
And unfathomable (...)

Scorched earth – (continued)

There's no defence for this
This 'once and for all'
Where victims have no rights
Or shelter from the fights
Picked by others

As babies are torn from their mothers

And we march into the abyss

Scorched earth – author's notes

'Scorched earth' was driven by the depths of inhumanity I have observed in current wars, where there is no hiding place from modern killing machines and the people that employ them continuously against the innocent and helpless, while laying waste to all else. If the cap fits.....

Those of us that can live, love, sleep, eat and raise families without being shot, bombed or shelled into fragments really have no excuse for silence, inaction or detachment in the face of such nihilism.

Whether the territory or blood feud has its roots in last week, month, year, decade or century, acquiescence in tit for tat mass killing implicates and condemns us all.

We have all seen this movie. It is time to de-legitimise and call a halt to this mindless failure of evolution.

Lifeboat of the lost - a poem about cruising

Another sail away
Plastic champagne
On the horseshoe stern
Ground hog day
Waiting to be fleeced
Will they ever learn?

The need to belong
Gangs new and old
In this playground
Are you gold,
Or simply blue?
So should I know you?

Territory is the thing
In this blinged out cage
Part of the cult
Must hog the best spot
No need to act your age
Better to have than have not (...)

Lifeboat of the lost – (continued)

The games begin
As the band plays on
Explorers circle Residents
Who know the form
In the days to come
There's no room for sentiment

Explorers know where they are
Residents barely a clue
The seven wonders sail by
While down in the casino
No one knew
Or wondered why

Nearing trip's end
Lifestyle Residents
Switch from smug to anxious
Must book another
With that low deposit
Plus 'free' on board spend

Or live with the shock
Of looking after themselves
With no coloured cruise card
Outside the gangs
With all their faux status
Left behind at the dock

Lifeboat of the lost – author's notes

Cruising has boomed in recent years, although it nearly went bust during Covid, while cruise lines now need to anticipate the approaching demise of their core baby boomer customer base.

However, if you go on longer cruises of more than two weeks in particular that core base is still there, wanting to keep many of the traditions alive. Meanwhile the cruise companies know precisely how to keep them committed.

As a late comer to cruising I have seen some of the changes happening, along with the differences between 'residents' who treat the ship as a home from home and 'explorers' who are eager to see more of the world, that some 'residents' have become quite jaded about.

'Lifeboat of the lost' is a wry look at the various territorial and hierarchical behaviours onboard, plus how the cruise lines feed the customer's future cruise habit, as an interesting study in human behaviour which I hope you enjoy.

Simply the worst - a poem about award ceremonies

It's bad enough
Isn't it though?
That 'insiders'
Have a need to self-congratulate
Be treated as special
For doing their job
While most of us
Gave up gold stars
At the school gate

It's worse
That they're boring
On the red carpet
Spouting scripts from a PR
Striking a pose
Fresh out of the 6 star
Limo or rented jet
Who do they think
They are?

It's beyond parody
That they preach
To mere mortal
As in us lesser folk (...)

Simply the worst – (continued)

With their carbon footprint
Like a volcano
And some just a headline away
From a scandal
Despite being so woke

It's time, beyond time
To call out this hubris
This alternative reality
Where 'celebrities' scoff lobster
Followed by baked Alaska
In aid of charity, apparently
While we all get on with it
Without fear or favour
Not needing to be flavour

Of the month

Simply the worst – author's notes

I have had my share of attending award ceremonies and have even won the odd niche award, but I have a problem with the whole concept.

Doing the job well should be recognition enough. Award criteria can be very subjective, while lobbying and compliance with fashionable group think can feature in the process.

Televised media and entertainment industry awards, that clog up the schedules in the autumn and winter, highlight the problem. The lobbying can be intense and the number of overlapping events e.g. for film and television, seems ridiculous. Meanwhile the virtue signalling from staging to speeches is frequently beyond parody.

Simply the worst – author's notes (continued)

In some cases the winners are great entertainers and some films or programmes are great entertainment, but that is all. No more meritorious than the output of so many unheralded people across the world, from the paddy fields to the factories, who just get on with it for a pittance.

'Simply the worst' is an invitation to scale down such self-serving and self-satisfied junkets, while upgrading the self-awareness.

What cold? - a poem about chilling detachment

We have no fear
Of heat or eat
As autumn blasts in
Cold reality is a stranger
To this presumptive elite

We have no fear
Of running out of money
Being cushioned by freebies
You must be a nobody
If you don't snag any

We have no fear
Of the public's disfavour
For such obvious corruption
Of rules never designed
To condone such behaviour

We have no fear
Of the sin of being old
Being inside the tent
As advisers and MPs
With none dying of cold (...)

What cold? – (continued)

In winter

Like them

What cold? – author's notes

I have a thing about politicians claiming that *'we are all in it together'*, implying shared pain in difficult times. The problem is that is almost never the case. Documenting the number of times politicians experience or are personally impacted by the consequences of their policies and decisions may well qualify as the smallest book in the world.

Persistent questions and analysis on that disconnect are very rarely followed through to conclusion by the established media, as they chase the next story.

Given how often U.K. politicians assume entitlement and see Westminster 'norms' as their lens on real life, the recent overlap of clothing and premium entertainment freebies for government ministers with the withdrawal of the winter fuel allowance for pensioners was not a surprise; but it was a particularly stark example.

What cold? – author's notes (continued)

What price free suits while cold pensioners lives are potentially at stake? Something I felt the need to crystallise in 'What cold?'

Nobody's collateral - a poem about child victims of acquiescence

You know infanticide is a crime right?
A war crime
Committed here and now
On your watch, all of you
In plain sight

Our small bodies smashed and buried
If all the pieces can be found
Or maimed for life
What passes for life
In such contested ground

Not that you care
In any way that's meaningful
Accepting weasel words
That cover up mass child killing
As simple war collateral (...)

Nobody's collateral – (continued)

It's time for accountability
As you all stand idly by
While order givers and takers
Execute scorched earth policies
And more abandoned innocents die

But some of us will survive
To haunt your future dreams
Pointing fingers across the abyss
As your assumed hegemony
Comes apart at the seams

And it's your turn

In our shoes

Nobody's collateral – author's notes

Along with non-combatant women and the old, innocent children are the major victims of war.

In most war histories the national leaders and armed forces are the story. One could be forgiven for thinking they were the majority presence in the battle zone, when of course they are the minority.

Children are inconvenient impediments to the prosecution of wars. They are written down as human shields when alive and collateral damage when dead and maimed, which is immoral, dehumanising, criminal and any number of other adjectives from the lexicon. 'Nobody's collateral' was written for such child victims and to remind us that every crime, even knowledgeable acquiescence in that crime, has consequences.

Message to Pasha - a poem about courage and commitment

I saw you training
With your comrades
To fight our battle
At one remove
Facing death
For a common cause
Without complaining

With no hesitation
Or self-regard
Changing your trade
From welder to killer
As needs must
To protect the innocent
Across your nation

Russia today
Is being resisted
Pushed back
And defeated
As aggressors must
To remind the world
That war does not pay (...)

Message to Pasha – (continued)

While your family
Are suffering too
All assumptions of normality
Which we take for granted
Replaced by privation
Destruction
And daily jeopardy

While we are concerned
About the price of bread
And energy inflation
Every day
Could be your last
In Ukraine's fight
With so much to be learned

By us

Message to Pasha - author's notes

Credit here to the Stacey Dooley fronted programme, "Ready for War?" which was broadcast on BBC Three in the first year of the Ukraine conflict, covering the training of a group of Ukrainian recruits, including a natural leader named Pasha.

This was powerful insight into how the British army was helping to prepare a Ukrainian citizen army for war against the Russian invasion. Everyone from welders to jewellers.

Pasha grew into leadership on the course, after leaving his job in the safety of Belgium, but was fatalistic about his future. The casualty rates at the front are very high and the Ukrainian female translator on the course was very emotional about likely fate of many recruits. At the time of writing Pasha's fate is not clear.

I wrote 'Message to Pasha' to honour his selfless commitment to defending his country and ultimately ours. Such people can teach us a lot.

Standing in the rain – a poem about electric vehicles

How did we get here?
Back to the 1950s
Where personal mobility
Is once again a luxury
For virtuous people
Apparently

As key workers despair
Back in the bus queue
Standing in the rain
Cold and wet
Splashed by their 'betters'
Once again

Driven by dogma
And one size fits all
Expensive technology
Just £40k to you guv
For an overweight box
With a floor full of batteries (...)

Standing in the rain – (continued)

Assuming you can charge it
Without a private drive
Or living in a city
Preferably in the South
Assuming we can generate
Enough electricity

With nuclear power
Needing four Hinckley Points
Oh didn't we say?
A can kicked down the road
To be picked up by others
On another day

A day too late
And £billions short
Of political ambition
While the vagaries of nature
Mock the hubris
Of wind farm promotion

Meanwhile in strip mines
In remote places
You never knew (…)

Standing in the rain – (continued)

People and nature
Are enslaved to the demands
Of the well-heeled few

It doesn't have to be like this
Using a mix of technologies
We have everything to gain
Before even the 'haves'
Their batteries flat as pancakes
Have to stand in the rain

Standing in the rain – author's notes

I have seen car ownership go full circle from the haves to the majority, before the current drift back towards being an option for the well-heeled only, as electric cars are deemed to be the future. As governments try to force the change public resistance is becoming inconvenient, but there is more going on than the headline objections.

The masses are becoming disenfranchised and pushed back towards standing in the rain at the bus stop by the high cost and impracticality of electric cars e.g. for those in most blocks of flats and terrace houses. This then becomes a problem for the well-heeled metro dwellers when they cannot source low paid workers who can afford to commute between jobs to serve them.
So welcome back to the 1950's. You have been warned.

What don't you understand? - a poem about ignorance and greed

About our small world

Where everyone can see everything
Through an eight-inch screen
And everything is closer
Than it has ever been

Except people

While our demise
Is fuelled by denial
Of issues critical
To our survival

And greed

The desperate scramble
To grab our share
While feigning charity
As if we care (...)

What don't you understand? – (continued)

Fuelling wars

For control
Of scarce resources
Under the cloak
Of market forces

Just so dumb

For homo sapiens
With scant realisation
Of obvious outcomes
From globalisation

The day will dawn

Sooner than wisdom
As the penny drops
When entitlement crumbles
And everything stops

What don't you understand? – author's notes

The people, animals and environment in the world have been interdependent for eons, even if they did not know it.

Now globalisation, mass travel and technology has shrunk our world in so many ways, while enabling us to see and measure our planetary impact and interdependence more quickly and easily.

However, denial is a ready and popular option for some. The scramble to grab more than our share of a shrinking cake is becoming more desperate, as the prospects for a soft landing recede with every mega storm.

'What don't you understand' grew from the suspicion that when the fruits of globalisation fail us we could be in for a hard stop.

Charity - a poem about loss of focus

Since when

Have the good needed to be great?
To be the CEO
Lauded and rewarded
Peers like their peers
Paid 'the market rate'

Since when

Was starvation a market?
Or being homeless
Or sick
Or abused
Come to that

Since when (...)

Charity – (continued)

Was this charity?
Rife with duplication
In competition
Used by many
As a career opportunity

So when

Will we stop this runaway train?
Where overheads matter
But cats get fatter
While others in need
Are left out in the rain

Assuming it does

Charity – author's notes

There are 170,000 registered charities in the U.K., some with significant overlap, e.g. 278 cancer charities at the last count.

Much good work is done by the 925,000 paid employees in the sector, plus many more volunteers, but it is open to question whether these many charities are as efficient as they could be in delivering funds and resources to those in need in their chosen sectors.

That is before considering that the average remuneration for the top 100 U.K. charity CEOs is around £170,000 per annum, for a role that is not a requirement of The Charity Commission. (*I don't remember such CEOs being a 'thing' in the past, but now they appear regularly in the media even for quite small charities*) All of which I thought might warrant an airing in 'Charity'.

This boat - a poem about being alive on BM45

Is our ark
For now
Older than we are
And likely to stay that way
A time capsule
Separated
From the issues of the day

All-consuming
As we manage the sails
Heavy stuff
For boomers like us
Creaking at the seams
Just like the rigging
Not in the first flush

Riding the wash
Of those in a hurry
In white plastic tubs
No timbers to shiver
On their party platforms
Only leaving the dock
In the absence of weather (...)

This boat – (continued)

Tomorrow it's our turn
To move back
To fast forward
To re-engage
With obligations
To meet offspring's expectations
Act our calendar age

Until next time

This boat – author's notes

We have been lucky enough to crew on tall ships and other classic boats, which involves adventure, escape to a different time and a lot of teamwork.

'This boat' was written after one of these trips on 'Pilgrim' in the west country, with a view to sharing the experience.

Life is hectic and sometimes it is good to step into a completely different space at a different pace.

Some of you might want to try it.

La Stazione – a poem about a social hub

You'll never be lonely
While sipping your latte
In La Stazione
Skinny or full fat
Not that you're fussy
When munching a toasty
Exchanging banter with Enzo
Or Max or Colin
Whether outside or in
The smiles are the same
Remembering your name
Always glad you came
Maybe to read a book
Or grab a Mocha to go
If you don't do slow
While those that do
Soak up the gossip
Perhaps about you
Or the council
For those who are political
Just as likely the children
Or their offspring
Little stars in waiting
After the ailments of course
Be they better or worse (…)

La Stazione – (continued)

Than last week's report
As a final resort
On a slow news day
In the real social network
Where anyone can play
With no phone necessary
In this cafe society
A little bit of Italy
In 'cold up north' Ilkley

La Stazione – author's notes

Time was when pubs were the social hub of the community, maybe with crisps or a pie, before they became 'gastropubs', before they then started disappearing.

Post Covid some of those remaining have retained QR codes and ordering via smartphone or tablet from the table. If you're lucky a human may serve you. or perhaps you have to queue at the pick-up station. Looking around you may see many with heads down in their devices, communicating apparently.

There is another way. Occasionally I visit Ilkley, where there is an Italian café, La Stazione, at the station entrance, that has taken on the role of unofficial community hub. The coffee and service are great, the (sometimes singing) waiters are fun and know your name Meanwhile the buzz of real conversation takes you back to a more engaged time.

I have written poems there, including this one.

Girl with a dog - a poem about life without limits

Walking the dog
A labradoodle I'm told
Between here and the park
Not a care in the world
Daydreaming
No need for a plan
Whether here
Or over the hills
Going to Uni
In a big city
Or further, who knows
With or without a man
Wherever the wind blows
Because it's all out there
To be discovered
With no hang ups
Aka experience
Wondering where your life went
Work hard but let it flow
A roller coaster for sure
But you have time
Time for patience
Things you cannot know
Because there's always more
As you throw the ball
And laugh at your pet (...)

Girl with a dog – (continued)

Live in the moment
Without introspection
With plenty of time
For a life well lived
Well remembered
For every decision
With no need for regret
So, go for it

Girl with a dog – author's notes

'Girl with a dog' was born out of a random event, becoming a word portrait of an everyday person and their opportunities.

It was early September. I was waiting for my wife to come out of a medical appointment when this young woman in a new looking university sweatshirt left a nearby house and made for the local park with her dog.

Totally mundane, but for some reason I thought back to my own student days, with the optimism and limitless horizons life offered and the determination to experience it all. Footloose and not a care in the world.

Hopefully it all worked out as well for her, her studies and the adventure of life beyond.

Common cause – a poem about calling their bluff

If war was a war crime
Would it give pause
To inadequates in dark glasses
Sacrificing us in their cause?

A self-declared elite
Such a tiny minority
Of men, mostly men
That could fit in a taxi

Or more likely a limo
With blacked out windows
Making orphans of children
Morphing wives into widows

What if we just say no?
Reach across the divide
Striking common cause with victims
The vast majority, on either side

Common cause – author's notes

There are more than 8,000,000,000 people on earth. So how on any given day do we allow just a handful of men, a taxi load, to perpetrate and perpetuate wars fought by the rest of us?

How?

It is not as though we have even met the 'enemy', or even those presumptuous 'leaders' that are so free with our lives while they shelter in their bunkers; entitled to demand we kill strangers, as the amorality of mass murder is indefinitely set aside.

But there is the opportunity for change.

New means of communication mean that zealots, opportunists and despots can no longer suppress the voices of reason and friendship indefinitely, as people talk and message each other across this small planet.
'Common cause' reflects the potential of that realisation.

Behind the façade – a poem about secrets and lies

Smart phones
Capture inconvenient truths
By the million
Secrets
Hiding under countless stones
Beyond the power of censorship
As victims of oppression
Are not alone
In their agony
Their pain exposed
For the world to see
Which was not the plan
Of those
Who would rather we didn't
See much at all
Except the image
They bought and paid for
And the people too
Role models
To me and you
Apparently

Behind the facade – author's notes

We are living through a communication revolution

Never before have normal people been so able to be aware and share awareness of facts and events that presumptuous elites would rather we didn't

Of course this is under threat as they try to crush such transparency and insert 'their truth' into those same channels. Right now they are playing 'whack a mole' and often losing, but we must stay vigilant.

I wrote 'Behind the facade' to highlight that we should enjoy this freedom and use it for good, while it lasts.

Wrong track – a poem about futile growth

How about those graphs?

Upwards to the right
The promise of more jam tomorrow
What we can't earn
We'll steal or borrow
To keep this show on the road

It's an article of faith

Supply must always chase demand
Boom the only alternative to bust
While 'experts' forecast
As they must
To keep this show on the road

In a broken dream (…)

Wrong track – (continued)

Where want is conflated with need
With 10,000 airliners on back order
And Venice going under
As wind-farms trade landscapes for power
To keep this show on the road

Time to wake up

To realise that the earth is finite
Betrayed by the chimera of 'net zero'
While politicians still talk growth
And first world voters pray for a hero
To keep this show on the road

But it's over

Wrong track – author's notes

Politicians often talk growth out of one side of their mouths and 'net zero' out of the other. Like 'green industries of the future', it's an oxymoron.
Even if wind turbines, solar panels, battery storage and more nuclear waste were the answers, their delivery depends on pollution generating global supply chains, horrendous strip mines and modern slave labour.
But it's what we want to hear, apparently. The promise of endless growth will keep politicians in place and consumerism on the road. So all we need is more supply, right? More goods, more transport, more resorts, more energy and on and on.
I wrote 'Wrong track' against this backdrop of kidology, while the real answers lie in reducing the demand to strip underdeveloped nations and the earth of finite resources, as the growth merry go round grinds to a halt.

Looking down – a poem about a slippery slope

We had it all
Or some did
For a time
At different times
Especially
In the north
The hemisphere
Of plenty
Unlike the south
Which
In the main
Bore all the pain
Of commodity

In those days

When we were smart
Or so we thought
Masters
Of our destiny
The universe
Even
As our numbers swelled
To 8 billion
Heedless
Humans (...)

Looking down – (continued)

Hellbent
On planetary
Destruction

As through the haze

We missed it
That moment
The first hive died
A silent dawn
That early thaw
A discarded mountain
Of fast fashion
A shimmering sea
Of micro plastic
As the best days
Of the have nots
Simply never
Arrived

Looking down – author's notes

This poem came about while assimilating the arguments raging around a climate conference

It has a dual theme.

One is the familiar denial of the developed nations that their prosperity has spawned a mountain of waste and insidious pollution, alongside their need to maintain their positions of economic dominance. Among the counter arguments from fast developing nations is that it is their turn to grow and they should not be held back.

The problem for both sides is that restraint is becoming non optional. There is no natural law that will keep the show on the road in the north, or that the southern hemisphere nations will get to enjoy their turn. 'Looking down' attempts to crystallise that challenge.

Night flight from Singapore - a poem about travel and perspective

Thrown together
Queuing, always queuing
Hurrying
Waiting
Anxious
Before we leave here
Zombies in the night
So many stories
Bobbing together
In the stratosphere
With time to kill
Time to sleep
Time to think
As lives coalesce
Briefly, up here
With more below
Exotic places
And people
We will never know
As we leave a trail
Across a silver moon
A muffled roar
More sensed than heard (...)

Night flight from Singapore – (continued)

A supranational presence
In their sky
For some routine
For others a dream
For some a curse
We are able to fly
For better or worse
In great circles
To everywhere
But as we return home
And sift through the mail
Were we really there?

Night flight from Singapore – author's notes

There is plenty of time to think during a long-haul night flight; especially if too cramped to sleep. While the hours drift by the flight tracker screen tells you which countries you are flying over and the progress of the journey.

As I stared at the screen on a flight home from Singapore I started to think about the lives of the people we were flying over; mostly very different from those of us on the plane. Perhaps some of them stirred in their sleep as we were overhead, vaguely aware of our passage; with others oblivious, conditioned to the nightly disturbance.

As we flew on, leaving our silver trail etched across their sky, 'Night flight from Singapore' was written somewhere between Pakistan and Iran.

Then we were home, suddenly back in our very work a day earth bound lives.

Clouds of infinity - a poem about the true place of humanity

Driving home tonight
Singing out loud
Strawberry fields forever
Across an endless plain
Under a big sky
While inky nebulae
Slid under a brass mirror
Who knows if they noticed me?
Cruising the heavens with disdain
For little things below
As the only things of scale
Anywhere
Quenching planets
Giving birth to stars
Filling space
Beside which our story pales
Which is an irony
As they are our ancestors
Made from base elements
Hydrogen, Oxygen, Water
Just like you and me
Slow to develop
They laugh longest (...)

Clouds of infinity – (continued)

While we scurry around
They simply wait
Condense and envelop
Silent and unnoticed

Except I did

Clouds of infinity – author's notes

I was driving home alone on a Sunday evening across a rural plain bordered by a ring of hills. It was autumn and the weather had been mixed, with bright sunshine and heavy rain showers. As the sun lowered to the horizon the sky was gradually changing from light blue to a brassy yellow.

I noticed a massive black cloud sliding under and across this backdrop. It dwarfed the surroundings and looked like the dark nebulae you see in photographs of deep space or the alien mother ship in the first 'Independence Day' film.

The normally busy road was empty into the distance. My thoughts strayed to the timeless nebulae that give birth to stars and how infinitely small and temporary I was, we are, by comparison. I wrote 'Clouds of infinity' as soon as I got home.

I'm not ready - a poem about perceptions of age

To shuffle off this mortal coil
Or pass away
Move to the wrong side of the grass
Or cash in my chips
At least not today

I have an appointment with Alan
About equity release
Who will move heaven and earth
To provide what I need
Before I rest in peace

Or I could meet Sun Life
Like my cheery neighbour
Who has a cheap plan
To help her family
Should the worst occur

Then before I check out
I could take Parky's advice
To do the right thing
And get a free gift
Which would be very nice (...)

I'm not ready – (continued)

I could write my will
And fund animal rescue
Or pay for some research
Perhaps funding clean water
Would be a good thing to do

Or I could turn off the tele
As I'm only seventy
Go do something new
Dodge the bullet
Until I'm good and ready

I'm not ready – author's notes

At one level the message in this poem is whimsical and obvious. Until it is you.

How many times are you asked for your age?

Official forms, job applications, medical records, banks….the list goes on. Which would be bad enough before the patronising, or treating you like an imbecile, kicks in; sometimes from people who would likely be challenged by mental arithmetic which you can do in your sleep.

"Do you have any need for special assistance?' is another favourite.
Ageism is rife. So I wrote 'I'm not ready' as an amusing antidote, but with a firm message.

www.ingramcontent.com/pod-product-compliance
Ingram Content Group UK Ltd.
Pitfield, Milton Keynes, MK11 3LW, UK
UKHW021441060625
6281UKWH00038B/331